L I

FOLK
TALES

LIMERICK FOLK TALES

RUTH MARSHALL

The
History
Press
Ireland

First published 2016

The History Press Ireland
50 City Quay
Dublin 2
Ireland
www.thehistorypress.ie

The History Press Ireland are a member of Publishing Ireland,
the Irish Book Publisher's Association.

British Library Cataloguing in Publication Data.
A catalogue record for this book is available from the British Library.

ISBN 978 1 84588 228 0

Typesetting and origination by The History Press

CONTENTS

ACKNOWLEDGEMENTS

My thanks go to all those who have walked alongside me, whether for longer or shorter stretches, on my journey through County Limerick's stories. It's all good, it all helped. In particular, my gratitude to: Carolanne Lamont and Iain Symes-Marshall for listening, reading, believing. Also Arran Purdie, Cat Lamont, Angie Pinson, Sinead Duignan and her children, Ann Mason for lifts into Limerick, Niamh Ní Lochlainn for sharing *bean feasa* stories, Anne O'Reilly for help with Irish spellings.

The children and teachers of the 1930s who gathered folklore and stories from their local areas for the Schools Folklore Scheme (1937–38). This is a truly fantastic resource.

To Criostoir MacCarthaigh, archivist, for advice, and the Irish Folklore Commission, UCD, for permission to draw from the Schools Folklore Scheme material; and for specific permission to include the story 'How the Forget-me-not Got Its Name' in its entirety in this book.

Mary Immaculate College Library and Limerick City Library local studies section.

Áine, sovereignty goddess and fairy queen, for bringing lightness and helping make writing this book such a delight.

All those who have told these stories before me. If you had not, I would not have found them today. Thank you to those who will read them and tell and retell again. This is how we keep stories alive.

ABOUT THE AUTHOR
AND ILLUSTRATOR

Born in Scotland, Ruth Marshall moved to Ireland thirty years ago.

Before settling in Ireland, she studied Archaeology and Botany at Glasgow University, worked as a folklore collector in the Scottish Highlands, and co-ran a wholefood shop.

In Ireland she joined a group of parents in founding a new school, which is now Raheen Wood Steiner National School in County Clare. She was a puppeteer, performing environmental puppet plays in schools and festivals around Ireland.

Ruth's son was born in 1989. This pivotal moment also brought about the birth of her storyteller self, as she began to create stories to entertain, soothe and ease adaptation to difficult circumstances.

Combining her interest in holistic living and spirituality with her skills in creative writing, she was editor and publisher of Ireland's holistic magazine, *Network Ireland*, for sixteen years. During this time she trained as a teacher of circle dance and soul-making and a facilitator of the Transformation Game, and became an energy healer and life coach. Crucially, while training as a Steiner kindergarten teacher, Ruth met Nancy Mellon, a pioneer in the work of storytelling as a healing art, and went on to do further courses with her in Ireland, the UK and Sweden.

Following her passion for keeping stories alive, Ruth has worked with all ages and abilities, from junior infants to retired older people. She taught creative writing for five years at ALFA Raheen Wood Steiner Secondary, and currently facilitates writing and personal development groups for adults. She believes in the healing power of the spoken word and derives great satisfaction from seeing others access their creativity and grow into more of who they really are.

As a storyteller and heritage specialist she visits primary schools through the Heritage in Schools Scheme, and gives storytelling and seasonal crafts sessions in museums, libraries, festivals.

Ruth's published works include *Celebrating Irish Festivals* (Hawthorn Press, 2003): a 'hands-on' guide to Celtic festivals with stories, crafts, recipes and games to help families and communities celebrate together, and *Clare Folk Tales* (The History Press, 2013): a collection of folk tales from County Clare. She also published poetry in journals and anthologies in the UK and Ireland.

www.ruthmarshallarts.weebly.com

INTRODUCTION

I was delighted to have the opportunity to write this book of folk tales from County Limerick and I have thoroughly enjoyed the process of finding, gathering and retelling stories, and illustrating them. Engaging with these stories has served to deepen my relationship with the landscape of County Limerick.

Limerick is the nearest city to where I live, across the Shannon in rural County Clare. It is where I would go for a big shop, for art and craft materials, to rummage through the charity shops, to see a film or go to theatre. As a city, Limerick is rich in culture and history, it has poetry, theatre, cinemas, colleges, university, art school, and it sits on the River Shannon. As a county, Limerick is also rich. It has good land, in the east it is part of the 'golden vale'.

The name Limerick has several possible origins: '*Luimneach*' in Irish means 'the flat area', which is quite a good description of the largely limestone plain of central County Limerick, with its few volcanic hills here and there. Others say it comes from '*Loimeanach*', meaning 'bare marsh' and refers to the Shannon shore near the city, or a 'place laid bare by horses'. Or perhaps it comes from '*Luimnigthe*', referring to the cloaks removed by warriors in battle by the river's edge.

The land was overseen by Áine, the queen of the Munster fairies, whose home was Cnoc Áine, one of the three fairy hills of County Limerick. Formerly one of the *Tuatha Dé Danann*, Áine was the goddess of sovereignty, who could confer, or retract, this gift at her will. There are stories of Áine's relationships with local rulers, Ailill

Ollam and Maurice, Earl of Desmond, and the children she bore them, including the poet-magician Gearóid Iarla. These stories resonated with me. I celebrated the way Áine fought back against her attacker, proving him unfit to rule the land. As a knitter, I identified with her in her guise as the woman who knits the green fabric of the world beneath the lake. So many riches, so many layers of truth. These stories are golden threads that weave a magical cloth.

As a balance, Donn Fírinne, king of the Munster fairies, had his residence nearby at Knockfeerina. Again there are stories of his interactions with local mortals as well as neighbouring fairies. Finn MacCool and his band of warriors hunted in the hills of County Limerick. Their names, grafted onto hills and townlands, tell us where they roamed. Later came saints, travelling through the county, leaving their blessings, or sometimes curses, behind them, as well as their names and stories. The fairies too are ever present, stealing away new mothers to nurture their young, or enticing musicians to play for their night-long dancing.

A tradesman who made himself most visible in the County Limerick tales was the tailor. The journeyman tailor travelled from place to place to ply his trade, and he brought his bit of know-how

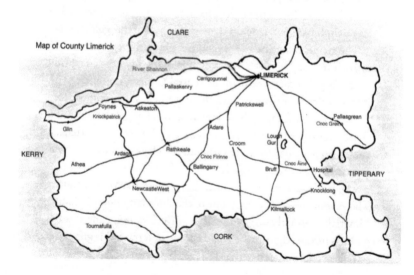

Map of County Limerick

problem solving with him to the households he stayed in, as well as the suits and shirts he made.

Another item of clothing, the apron, started to show up in different stories in curious ways. Biddy Early, Clare's famous wise woman and healer, makes an appearance, as does Limerick's own *bean feasa*, Joan Grogan. Joan would find her cures by travelling out of her body while in a trance state, then instruct the woman of the house to hold up her apron to receive whatever would fall into it. In other tales, giant women shape the landscape by carrying bits of mountains in their aprons, and men wear aprons to sow seed. The apron motif fascinated me: this practical garment that protects the wearer and has so many uses. I noticed that I often wore one of my own colourful aprons when I sat at my laptop at the kitchen table, typing up stories or drawing story characters – many of them in their aprons.

Where there are wise women and old wives, there are also fools: holy fools who make good. In this collection, you will find not Jack, but Tadhg, Pat and Sean, each of whom ends up surprising his mother, and proving he has his own kind of wisdom. There is hope for us all.

I hope that in having found and retold these stories, I am doing what I can to help keep them alive. In turn I hope that in reading them you will also find a deepening respect and relationship with the land and the people of County Limerick. Perhaps you will be encouraged to visit places featured in the stories. If you do, I am certain you will find magic, mystery and more tales to share.

Ruth Marshall, 2016

1

THE LIMERICK

Limerick has been home to many poets, and some claim it is the source of the well-known popular verse form that bears its name. We all know the Limerick's short, punchy form: five lines, rhyming AABBA, with a humorous and often bawdy subject matter. The Maigue Poets certainly used the form, and it was often followed by a line from a popular song, 'Will you come up to Limerick', but it was the English writer Edmund Lear who popularised it in his books of nonsense verse in the nineteenth century.

Limericks are fun: they have a familiar rhythm and an easy rhyme scheme. They make us laugh. Children make them up spontaneously, so we know you don't need to be a gifted poet to create one. The Limerick is a people's poem. So here goes: my attempt at a Limerick.

> There are riches more precious than gold,
> Such as stories that need to be told,
> Full of legends and tales
> From the hills and the dales.
> Now the book simply needs to be sold.

2

THE TAILOR

The journeyman tailor was an important character in the old times. He would travel from place to place, bringing his tools and his fabrics with him for the making or mending of a suit of clothes. He would stay with a household while he worked for them, and rely on their hospitality, and he would bring news and stories with him. As a stranger in a household, he might notice what others had simply taken for granted, so in many stories it is the tailor who sees that there is something strange going on when, for example, an old woman keeps coming back asking for coals from the fire. It is often the tailor who knows how to make changes to restore the natural order of things.

THE TAILOR AND THE FAIRY CHILD

A farmer and his wife lived together in an old mill with their baby son, just nine months old. They had a good life; all three were happy and healthy and the work on the farm was going well.

One day while the man was out in the fields, the wife went out to the stream to fetch a pail of water, leaving her son fast asleep in his basket. When she came back, the child was screaming so loud you'd think the world was coming to an end. His face was turning blue and when she looked closer, it seemed that he had shrunken and shrivelled. What had happened to her happy boy? She picked the child up to nurse him, but he kicked and turned, shrieking all the more, and would not settle in her arms. Was there something terribly wrong with him? She could see no sign of anything, but determined to keep a close eye on him as the day went on. However, after that day, the child grew not an inch taller, but stayed skinny and gaunt. He did not crawl on the floor, nor babble and knock over blocks like a normal child. All day long he only lay in his basket, crying and waving his wiry arms in the air.

A tailor, Connolly by name, came by looking for work. The farmer had work for him, so he agreed to stay the week the work would take. A bed was made up for him, and he set to his sewing. The first day, as he sat and sewed, he noticed the child's constant whimpering. 'What is the matter with the boy?' he asked. The wife told him how her son had changed the day she had left him to fetch water. 'I should never have left him alone!' she cried, blaming herself for the boy's troubles. Connolly puzzled over this: why would the child suddenly change?

A few days later both farmer and wife set off for the market in Newcastle West, leaving the tailor in charge of the house and the child, still grizzling in his basket. They had hardly left the house when a voice called out, 'Hey, Connolly!'

Connolly looked around. As there was no one in the house save himself and the child, he went back to his stitching. But the voice called again, 'Come here, Connolly!' The tailor was afraid. Could it really be the sickly child who was calling him? What should he do?

Connolly went over to the basket. The sickly child was sitting up with a hideous grin on his face. 'Can you keep a secret?' it asked.

'Eh, I can,' stammered the tailor, wondering what might happen next.

'Very well!' said the child, leaping out of the basket and taking down a fiddle that hung over the fireplace. The child then danced around the kitchen, playing jigs and reels, and it was fine music he played, so the tailor could not help but dance along with him. He played tune after tune until they heard the farmer and his wife returning from the market. The child quickly hung up the fiddle, jumped back into the basket, and began to whimper.

Connolly drew the farmer and his wife aside. 'Might I have a word with ye?' he asked.

'What is it, man? Is there something wrong?'

'It is the child,' says the tailor. 'He is not your own child at all, but a fairy, lying there in his place.'

'Is there anything we can do to get our own son back?' cried the wife.

'Leave it to me,' says Connolly, 'and I will get him to give you back your son. But stay out of the room while I do this, for it might upset you to watch.'

Connolly went back into the room, taking a shovel with him. He took up a shovelful of red coals from the fire, and came over to the basket.

'Get out of there now before I roast ye alive!' cried Connolly brandishing the red-hot shovel before the fairy child's face. 'Bring back the son of this house and be gone from it yourself!'

The 'child' leapt from the basket and, shrieking like a banshee, went running from the house. Although they chased him down the road, the tailor, the farmer and his wife could not catch him.

When they returned to the house, there was their own smiling child sitting up in the basket, round and plump and singing happily to himself. He reached up his small hands towards his mother. The woman lifted him from the basket and held him to her breast, sniffing his soft hair and calling all the sweet names a mother calls her beloved child.

There was no more crying in that household. The child grew tall and learned to speak and stand, and was the shining light of his parents' lives from that day on.

Connolly the tailor finished his work there later that evening. Next day he would be moving on to the next-door neighbours, and he would have another story to tell when he got there.

THE MISSING BREAKFAST

The following morning, the people of the house were still sleeping soundly when Connolly gathered his things and was ready to leave. There was no breakfast ready for him, but surely the next-door neighbours would give him some food when he arrived there. It was not so far to the next house, and the walk would only help him work up an appetite.

When he reached the neighbours' farm, they'd been up already since the cock had crowed. Their breakfast was long past, and the dishes all washed up and the pans hanging up gleaming. They did not offer the tailor a bite to eat, so by the time ten o'clock came by, his stomach was crying out for food. What could he do?

Connolly called the woman of the house and asked her for a lighted candle. When she brought it, he took it outside and went walking back and forth along the road he had come. The woman followed him, and at last she asked him, 'What are you looking for out on the road with a lighted candle in the broad daylight?'

'I was looking for my breakfast. Somehow I must have missed it between that other house and yours. I was looking to see was it out here on the road and I had passed it by.'

'Come on away back in with you and I will put on a pot for you,' said the woman of the house, laughing as she blew out the candle. 'You only had to tell me you were hungry. You will not starve while you are staying in my house.'

She brought Connolly back into the kitchen and cooked up a fine breakfast for him. Three good meals a day he had while he was staying there, and another story to tell when he moved on.

COALS AND BUTTER

Another time a journeyman tailor was staying on a farm while he was making a suit of clothes. The man and woman of the house were going to market in Abbeyfeale one day to sell their butter, eggs and chickens. They left the tailor sitting by the kitchen table, busy at his work. 'Would you just keep an eye about the place, and let us know anything that happens while we are gone?'

'Of course,' says the tailor, and he got on with his work.

He was stitching away at the table when the door of the kitchen opened and in came a small round old woman with a large white apron on her. 'Would you give me a coal from your fire, for my own has gone out and I have nothing to light it with?'

The tailor did not know the woman, but he saw no harm in it. He picked up the iron tongs and took out a hot coal and gave it to the woman.

The woman thanked him for the coal and she was gone. He did not watch to see which way she went nor how far from the house.

Only once she was gone, did the tailor wonder what the woman was about. Then he took up his tongs and took out a single coal from the fire. He took his coal down to the end of the hall and put it in a large pot. That pot was used for cooking up scraps for the pigs and poultry, and there was a bit of water in it.

He went back to his stitching at the table. It wasn't long until the small round old woman with a large white apron on her came back. 'Mister, can you give me another coal. The one I got before went out.'

The tailor gave the old woman a second coal. When she had gone, he took another coal and added it to the pot in the hall, and placed a lid on it.

A third time the old woman came asking for a coal. The tailor gave her a red coal, and then he put one more coal in the pot in the hall and covered it up.

When the man and woman of the house returned from the market, they asked the journeyman tailor what he had seen that day.

'I saw much that puzzled me,' he said. 'But first, can I ask you a question? How are ye getting on with the farm here? Are ye having much luck with it?'

The farmer replied, 'To be honest with you, things are not going so well for us here.'

'Is there a problem with the milk or the butter?' asked the tailor.

'Yes,' said the wife. 'The cows are never giving the milk we should be getting, and there is hardly any butter to speak of.'

Then the journeyman tailor told them, 'A very strange thing happened today when you were away. An old woman came to the house three times looking for a coal from the fire. I gave her the coals, but I thought there was something odd. So I took the precaution of taking a coal myself, and adding it to your pot in the hall. I think whatever has been wrong on the farm, you will find it in there.'

When the wife took the lid off the pot in the hall, she found it filled to the brim with butter!

The tailor had guessed the old woman's trick to steal the butter, and blocked the spell. There was no more trouble with the milk and butter on that farm.

And the journeyman tailor, well, now he had another story to tell on his evenings by the fire in every house he visited.

THE TAILOR AND THE HARES

On May Day morning, people always needed to be wary lest someone steal away their butter.

There was a tailor who lived alone in a small cottage beneath a hill. One morning in May an old woman came knocking at his door. She asked for a coal from his fire and, not thinking what day it was, he gave her the coal, and away she went. But once she was gone, he thought to take a coal and put it in a pot of water. A few minutes later the old woman was back, asking for another coal. Again he gave her one, but took one himself as soon as she had gone. That was how it went on, until the whole fire was gone, and yet still the old woman had no hold over him with her spell. Next she came back and took out a tin of ointment from a hole in the fireplace. When she rubbed this on her face, at once she turned into a hare, and was gone, running out the door.

The tailor opened the tin, and rubbed some of the ointment on his own face. Soon he was racing out the door and after the other hare. He followed her to a field full of hares, there must have been hundreds of them, all leaping around a man on horseback. There were cows there too, his neighbour's cows, and some of the hares were milking them.

The horseman suddenly called out, 'Stop! There is a stranger among us here!'

The hares went racing in all directions, and the tailor ran for home as fast as he could go, chased by the horseman who managed to slap him on his left cheek with his whip. When he reached home, the tailor rubbed the ointment on his face, and became a man again. The place where the horseman's whip had caught him remained covered with grey fur ever since that day.

TAILOR SPELLMAN'S SPELL

There was a tailor called Spellman who lived close to Knockainy Hill. Every morning he used to go walking up the hill. He would speak a few words there on top of the hill. Then he'd take out his needle and he would point it towards each of the points of the compass: to the north, the south, the east and the west. Then he'd walk around, still holding out his needle, until he'd done a whole circle. When he'd finished that, he'd put the needle back in his case and down the hill he'd go, back home and get on with his work for the day.

Every day he did his morning walk up the hill, and there was no other tailor who could enter Knockainy. If a journeyman tailor was heading that way, something would get in his way, and he would have to turn back. That was his way of protecting his business.

THE TAILOR'S SECRET

There was a tailor who lived in Knocklong who was always busy. People would go to him by preference because, as well as being a fine tailor, he was also a great storyteller. People would travel a long way to get this tailor to make their clothes because of his fascinating tales. Other tailors would visit too, because they thought he had a 'charm' that helped him make clothes so neat and tidy. They all wanted to know what his secret was. There were a lot of tailors around and every one of them was looking for that bit of an edge over the others.

One day the tailor got very sick and he realised that his time was coming. He sent a message out to all the other tailors in the district, saying he was on his deathbed and he had no wish to take his secret with him to the grave.

Word travelled fast and before long all the tailors within 50 miles were crowded into the tailor's shop. They waited, chatting among themselves until the tailor was ready to reveal the secret of his trade.

The old tailor sat up in his bed and declared, 'My friends and fellow tailors, I believe I am not long for this world. Before I take my final breath and reach the gates of the world beyond, I would like to tell you something that has served me well through all my years of tailoring. I have always had plenty of trade, and there is a good reason for that. Come close now, for I feel my strength is leaving me.'

The tailors all gathered in close around the bed, holding their breath, desperate to hear the secret of his success.

'Here is my advice to you,' the old tailor continued. 'Whenever you sew on a button, always tie a knot at the end of your thread ...'

All the tailors gasped, as the old man closed his eyes and lay his head back on his pillow, taking the real secret with him to the world beyond.

SOURCES

'The Fairy Child', 'The Missing Breakfast': NCFS 514:325-7; John Aherne, Kilbeheny, County Limerick. Kilbeheny (C) School
'Coals and Butter': *Irish Life and Lore: Jim Lane & Denis Broderick* – part 2
'The Tailor and the Hares': NCFS 492:164-166; Ned Leahy, Tournafulla. Collector: Mary Mulcahy, Tournafulla. Gleann Gort School, Newcastle West
'Tailor Spellman's Spell': NFC 1799:116, 1971
'The Tailor's Secret': NCFS 516:459; John Dooley, Grange, County Limerick. Grange School, County Limerick

3

OLD WIVES AND WISE WOMEN

JOAN GROGAN

Just as County Clare has Biddy Early, renowned as a wise woman throughout the whole country, so County Limerick has Joan Grogan. She lived in West Limerick, near the Kerry border, and had a reputation as a healer and seer. Here are some of the stories told about her and her abilities.

How Joan Found Her Power

Joan Grogan was born in a small, modest house in the townland of Athea, near the border with County Kerry. She seemed happy enough, was a lively child, and there was no sign in her early years of any particular ability that would set her apart from others. She grew up among the girls and boys of the district, and joined in their sport and play like any other girl.

When she was around 20 years old she set off with a crowd of other young people to a wake. It was already dark when they set off and the group stayed close together, laughing and joking on their way. But when they crossed a stream the party split, some leaping across quickly and racing ahead while others took their time crossing the water. So none of them noticed that Joan was missing. The first and faster group just thought she was coming up behind with the other party; while the second group thought she had gone ahead with the first.

By the time they all met up again at the wake, they noticed that Joan was not among them. They thought little of it, laughed at how each had thought she was with the others. 'She must have decided to go home early,' they said, or 'Joan probably changed her mind and went to see her auntie.'

No one was concerned that Joan was not with them, nor thought any harm had come to her. But the next morning, there was a very strange story on everyone's lips, telling what had befallen Joan Grogan. Joan herself had no memory at all of that night, from setting out with her friends for the wake until she woke up in the strangest of places. She awoke in the morning out of a deep sleep, but was as surprised as anyone might be to find herself sitting up on the roof of her own house, up on the top of the chimney pot! How she had got there she couldn't begin to wonder, but because she herself laughed at the absurdity of it, everyone else treated it as a strange joke.

After that night Joan began to have epileptic fits from time to time. She had also suddenly developed a kind of second sight, for now she knew things about other people that no one else could have known. When she was having a fit, Joan would somehow travel out of her body and see things that she had no way of knowing. Some began to fear Joan for the strange power she had and they called her a witch. But to others, she was a wise woman who could help them with cures for diseases of man and beast.

The news of her abilities spread and people came to her from far and near for help. Joan found that she could bring on a fit or trance at will by drinking a little whiskey. When she visited the house of a sick person, she would often tell the woman of the house to go and open the door and hold out her apron. Then a sprig of herbs would fall into the outstretched apron. When these were boiled in goat's milk, they were given to the patient to drink.

They say that Joan cured several people whom the doctors had given up as hopeless cases, and once she even raised a man who had been dead for twenty-four hours and he lived for a further five years after that!

Meat for the Table

As often happened to women with knowledge of healing, the priests took against Joan, claiming her powers came from an evil source, and warned people to stay away from her. They went so far as to excommunicate Joan, although she was welcomed back into the fold before she died.

When Joan was visiting a neighbour one day, there was only a few potatoes and a jug of buttermilk when the family sat down for dinner. Joan said aloud, 'It is a pity there is no meat for your dinner.'

'You are right there,' said the man of the house. 'It is indeed, but what can we do?' Joan went up and opened the back door. She held up her apron stretched between her two hands. The next thing you knew, there was a joint of roast beef came falling down into her apron. Joan brought the joint of meat to the table, saying, 'Here is a fine joint of meat for your dinner!' and with that, she left the house, so that they could enjoy their meal. The meat was hot, as if it had just come out of the oven, and the aroma was rich and made their mouths water. But not one of them would touch so much as a mouthful of it, no matter how delicious it smelt. When Joan had gone, the woman of the house took the meat outside, threw it away across the fields, where none of their animals could find it, and left it there for the crows or foxes. Perhaps they had listened to the priest when he spoke against Joan in the church on Sunday, but they did not trust the source of the meat and were afraid to tempt fate by eating it.

A Cure

Joan worked at one time for a man in Glenamore. In the house there was a young man who suffered with polyps in his nose. When he asked her could she find a cure for him, she put herself into a trance, and whilst she was 'out of herself' she spoke to those present and gave them instructions on what to do for the cure.

She told a woman in the house to go out and milk a certain goat belonging to her master, which would be found at the top of the boreen near the house. She said she must watch out, for the goat would get its leg twisted three times, and try to spill the milk. Joan told her that if the milk should be spilt three times the cure would not work. She said that if any of the milk were saved, it was to be boiled and certain herbs to be sprinkled in it. She told them where to find these herbs, which was on the bed where the patient usually slept.

The woman went out and did as Joan instructed. She milked the goat, and the milk was spilt twice, but saved the third time. She found the herbs lying where Joan had said and put them in the milk to boil. The drink was given to the young man and he recovered completely.

Joan would tell the woman of the house to watch the pot well as she boiled the herbs in the milk, as the colour of the leaves could foretell the fate of the sick person. If the herbs should turn green, the patient would surely recover; whereas if the herbs turned brown, then they would die.

Stolen Butter

Home-made butter is yellow as gold and every bit as precious. People used to steal a neighbour's butter, if they could. They would put a piseóg on it: a spell of some kind, that would mean your butter would go to them, and you would have none, despite all your work at churning.

Joan Grogan was sent for one day by a farmer's wife. Day after day, despite hours of churning, she could not turn her milk into butter. Everyone believed that someone, perhaps even a neighbour, had put a charm on it and was stealing away their butter.

Joan arrived, and having drunk her glass of whiskey, she fell down writhing on the floor. When her limbs became still, she lay on the floor, her face as pale as if she herself had died. Then suddenly she sat bolt upright and began to give orders that they should now start the churning. While they were busy with churning, Joan called for the sock of an iron plough to be brought into the kitchen and set on the fire to heat.

Despite all the best efforts of the woman of the house and her maids, busy at the churn, still the butter would not come.

Joan called out, 'Now, it is time, you need to be watching that house up on top of the hill.'

Joan took up the fire tongs, removed the plough sock from the fire, and plunged it into the churn. Steam filled the dairy, with the sizzling sound of hot iron in cold liquid.

The woman and her maids ran outside to watch the house up the hill. And what did they see but the neighbour woman running out of her own door, waving her hands in the air, her feet stamping. They could hear her screaming, 'Stop it! I beg you, make it stop! I swear I will give you back every bit of butter I took from you, if you will just stop burning me!'

It was the neighbour on the hill who had been charming away the dairy woman's butter. But now that Joan had exposed her for her trick, she kept her word and gave the dairy woman two big firkins of good butter, and she never interfered with the butter-making again.

Well, Well, Well

There were two men digging in a garden. After a time they needed to take a break and have a bite to eat. Once they had eaten, the pair sat down to take a smoke of their pipes. One of the men fell asleep on the ground, while the other took up his spade again and returned to his work.

Suddenly the sleeper was rudely awakened by a blow to the head. He sat up with a start and, seeing a big stone close by, accused the other of hitting him with the rock. 'If I did, I did not know I did,' said the other man, who had simply been working away. The man had not seen the stone at all.

Later that night, back at his home, the man complained of a terrible pain in his head. His wife sent for Joan Grogan to come and help.

Joan put herself into a trance, and then she told the man that it was the ghost of a dead man who had struck him. She gave detailed instructions of what he must do to restore things to a balance again.

He was to visit three holy wells; he was to walk round each well three times; he was to take a handful of mud from each well, place it on his side, and then return it carefully to the spot it had come from. She also told them to give three alms for the good of the man's soul that had harmed him and for the good of the man's soul that did him good.

The man's family did all that Joan instructed. The man was so unwell that he had to be carried on a table to the first well. By the time he visited the second well, he was able to be brought in an ass and car. The man's health continued to improve and he rode to the third well on his own horse.

They had done all that Joan had said, and the man was feeling quite well again. How she knew, they never learned, but Joan Grogan came to the door, and told them, 'You have still to give the alms. I warn you, the cure is not complete until that is done too.'

When that was done, the man was back to his old self again, thanks to Joan Grogan.

The Place of Skulls

A man and his nephew lived near Newcastle West. One day the nephew grew sick. The doctor could find no cure so the man called to Joan Grogan for her help. It was late in the evening when he knocked at Joan's door.

'Who is this from the place of skulls, knocking at my door?' called Joan. She had seen that the uncle lived next to the church-yard, where the grave diggers piled any unearthed bones on the walls of the monastery ruins.

The man told her of his nephew's sickness. Joan listened and then told him he must follow her instructions to the letter, if his nephew was to live. He agreed.

She told him he was to go to the ruined church at the stroke of midnight on the Friday night following the next full moon. He was to take a skull and bring it home with him. He must scrape small shavings from the skull into a small pot of water and bring this to a boil over the fire. All the time he was doing this he was to speak aloud the name of the person who he wished would die instead of his nephew seven times.

When such instructions are given, usually it is the name of a sick or elderly person, close to death, that is spoken. Someone who is grateful for their end to be hastened. But not so, in this case.

The uncle discussed the matter with his own son and with his agreement, he spoke the name of his son's wife as the one he wished would die in his nephew's place.

Whatever the morality of this particular cure, the nephew recovered, and lived to a great old age, without ever knowing the price of his recovery. The uncle died suddenly a year to the day after his visit to the place of skulls and his own son died the following year.

BIDDY EARLY

Biddy Early's Message

Back in the old times, people didn't have a clock to tell the time with. They relied upon the sun and the needs of their animals to tell them what time of day it was.

Near Ballyallinan, a girl called Margaret Lister lived with her mother and sister, and they had a servant girl called Mary living in the house.

One morning Margaret called Mary to let her know it was 'cow time,' or maybe even later than that. The two of them took up their pails and went out to milk the cows. While they were busy at their work, and singing their songs to keep the cows happy, a man came riding by on a grey horse. With great curiosity, he stopped alongside the girls and watched them. After a while, he asked why they were up so early.

Margaret had been taught not to answer a stranger's questions, but she spoke to the horseman. 'But it is not early at all. The cows need milking, so it's time to be up and working.' When the man rode on, the girls carried on with their work, then went back inside.

That night Margaret woke up around midnight, and got a fright when she saw the strange man outside her window. The following night he was there again at midnight.

The next day, Margaret did not feel well, and could not get out of her bed. When she hadn't improved by next morning, her mother was troubled. She told her neighbour about Margaret, and was told, 'You need to talk to Biddy Early, and the sooner the better, for Margaret's sake.'

Biddy Early was a healer in Clare. It was a long way to go, so they sent a message instead. When Biddy's message came back, the mother was told, 'You need to go to the door and hold out your apron. Whatever herbs fall into it, you boil that up and strain it off. Give the juice of it to Margaret to drink.'

The mother did that and, sure enough, a bunch of herbs fell into her apron. She boiled up the brew and spooned it into Margaret's mouth. After a short while, Margaret was right as rain again.

Biddy Early and the Butter

There was a woman named Mrs Walsh and she was in terrible trouble because she couldn't make her butter right. She had spent all day at the churning, and all she had to show for it was sour milk. No fat golden lumps had formed at all. When she told her neighbour what was happening, the kind neighbour told her it sounded like there was a *piseóg* on it. She told her that Biddy Early would surely help get rid of the *piseógs*.

Mrs Walsh told her son, Pat, to get the horse and cart ready and to drive with her to Clare. Poor Pat had a terrible morning in the mud and rain, trying to catch the horse. He slipped and fell, and ended up covered from head to toe in muck. He lost his patience and cried out, 'Bad luck to you, Biddy Early, if it wasn't for you, I'd not be run ragged this morning!'

They were a good few hours on the road before they reached Biddy's house. Biddy was there waiting at the door and before a word of greeting was said, she said, 'Did you hear that nice wish your son gave me this morning while he was chasing the horse in the mud, Maggie Walsh? Bad luck he wished me!'

Poor Mrs Walsh got a fright when she heard this. She was afraid that Biddy wouldn't help her after Pat's ill wish. Pat, who was bright red with shame, apologised, 'I am sorry Missus. I didn't mean it. I was just so mad with the horse.' Biddy waved him away, 'Never do that again,' she said, 'and don't worry, I will help your mother get her butter back.'

Biddy told Mrs Walsh to go home and search in the ditch between her land and her neighbour's. 'You will find a green bottle hidden there. Take it and smash it into pieces. After that your next churning will bring plenty of butter.'

They thanked Biddy, got back in the trap and set off for home.

Next morning they searched all along the ditch. At last they found something in the fork of a blackthorn bush. It was a large green glass bottle full of some foul liquid. Mrs Walsh took up that bottle and threw it with a vengeance against the wall. The bottle smashed to smithereens, and whatever was in it smelled like rotten eggs. The next day, Mrs Walsh was back at her churning, and the golden lumps of butter were there for her in abundance!

Anna Cliar and Biddy Early

On Cnoc Áine Hill there lived a woman called Anna Cliar. They called her that because on Midsummer's Eve, when everyone would light a *cliar* or torch, hers would be the first one lit. Anna Cliar lived in a grand palace, but you wouldn't see it with everyday eyes, not unless you looked through Anna Cliar's ring. All you would see would be a plain green field.

On Misummer's Eve, and most Sunday evenings in the summertime, there would be a dance held in the field at the bottom of the hill. The young folk would all be there, dressed in their best. Anna Cliar would be there and she would be the finest of them all in her white dress.

There was a man around there who had only one son and his son was precious to him: he helped on the farm and would inherit it when his time came. One evening that boy went along to the dance and didn't Anna Cliar set her eye on him? She was looking so fine that night, and she went all out to get his attention. He was

so caught up in her charms that he danced with her one dance
after another, without looking at the other girls. He was lost,
looking into her eyes as they danced together, when suddenly she
swept him up into the air. The next thing he knew he was flying
through the air and away to Anna Cliar's fabulous palace. All the
other young people were having fun, dancing or talking together,
and no one noticed that he had disappeared.

That night, when he did not come home, his father was worried.
He was still not home in the morning, or the next day, and the father
looked for him all around the area. He stopped and asked everyone
he met if they had seen his boy, who had not come home from the
dance, but no one knew where he was. A year had almost passed
when he met a woman who suggested, 'You should go and see Biddy
Early. She'll be able to tell you where he is and how to get him back.'

When he got to Biddy's house, Biddy was burning up with a
fever. There was a little girl there to care for her while she was sick.
'Oh my! It is your only son you've lost and I can tell you where he
is,' said Biddy. 'He is away with Anna Cliar! Anna Cliar has him
up in Cnoc Áine. But here am I sick myself with the fever and I am
sorry, but I can do nothing to help you today.'

The man was disappointed; he had come so far to find no help
at all. He was turning sadly for home, when the little girl said,
'Give me your book, mother, and I will go with him.'

'You will not, child. You haven't got the power to face Anna
Cliar,' said Biddy.

'This is the only chance he has to get his son back. A year and a
day is almost gone. You must let me try.'

'I suppose you are right,' said Biddy. 'Now here's what you must do.
Go and get feathers from the hens and rub those on yourself. Take
my stick and my book with you, and may you have good luck with it.'

The girl did as Biddy said and they set off for Cnoc Áine.
Halfway up the hill, there was a big flat flagstone. The girl rapped
on the stone three times with Biddy's stick. 'This is the door to
Anna Cliar's palace,' she told the man. The rock lifted up and
Anna Cliar came out and stood before them. 'What brings you
knocking at my palace door? What do you want?'

'You have this good man's son in there, and I have come to get him back,' said the girl, holding up Biddy's book between her and Anna Cliar.

'What have you got in that book?'

'If I were to tell you that, you would know as much as I do myself!' With that, she came up so close to Anna Cliar that their noses were almost touching. Now Anna Cliar could smell the hens' feathers and her face twisted with disgust. Whatever power was in them I don't know, but Anna Cliar turned and ran, leaving the door to her palace open. A few minutes later, the lad came out into the light of day and went home with his father.

Not All Can Be Saved

Despite her great insight and abilities, there were times when even Biddy Early could not save the life of a sick person. There was a man around Kilfinnane who had a son who had been two years on his sickbed, attended by two different doctors. Nothing they had tried could help at all. The neighbour said, 'You must go to Biddy Early in Clare. She's the only one who can help him now.'

The man didn't believe in Biddy and her cures. He thought it was all superstition and old wives' tales, but to please his wife he said he would go. 'You know I have no faith in all that, but if I don't go, and he dies, I will be feeling sorry that I didn't try everything to save him.'

He did not want Biddy to know who he was, so as he travelled to Clare he made up a sorrowful tale to spin her. In his story, he was a poor man with a house full of hungry children and only one cow. The cow was sick and he feared that it would die soon.

When he arrived at Biddy's door, she was there waiting. 'Don't waste your breath telling me that tale you cooked up on the way. I know you have no sick cow. It is your own son who is sick and lies dying in his bed.'

The man was amazed at this proof that her fabled powers were real. 'How can you know that?'

'Oh, I know your house as well as I know my own,' said Biddy with a kind smile, 'and I know your troubles'.

'So can you help me? Can you save my son?' he asked her, with a new respect for the wise woman.

'I am sorry,' said Biddy. 'There is nothing I can do for you. Your son was too fond of his late nights and his drink. Among his cronies there was a fool, and one night he struck your son as they were crossing a field. There is no cure for anyone struck by the fool.'

As tears slipped down the father's face, Biddy took his hand and said, 'His time is close, but if you leave now, and make no delay on the road, you will be home in time to say goodbye.'

The man left at once, but he did not forget to thank Biddy for her kind words. When he reached home, his son was taking his last breath.

A Deathbed Message

All her days Biddy Early gave people whatever help she could with her insights and her cures. All that time the priests spoke out against Biddy from their pulpits, declaiming that she was a witch. They told the people not to give directions to anyone seeking Biddy's house, because her powers came from an unholy source.

Biddy lived to a great old age, and when at last she lay dying, she sent for the priest. He refused to attend her. Biddy sent for him a second time, and again he stubbornly refused. She sent a third message, saying she could not die easy in her bed until she had seen the priest. She said she had information to share that would benefit both priests and ordinary folk. This time the priest came to her deathbed. No one knows what mysteries Biddy told the priest. Whatever it was, it must have made some impression, for there were twenty-seven parish priests in attendance at her funeral, one from each parish in Clare.

The Sunday following Biddy's funeral, the priest announced to his congregation, 'We thought we had a demon amongst us in poor Biddy Early, but we had a saint and we did not know it.'

SOURCES

'How Joan Found Her Power', 'Place of Skulls': NFCS 485:309-311.
Mr Sheehan. Collector: William Danaher, Gortnagros, Athea, County
Limerick

'A Cure': NFCS 491:260-261. Mrs N. Riordan of Monagea. Collector:
Mary Ahrerne, Monagea, Newcastle West, County Limerick. Scoil:
Monagea (C)

'Well, Well, Well': NFCS 480:386, Glin Girls School, Glin, Limerick
NFCS 485: 309-311. Mr Sheehan. Collector: William Danaher,
Gortnagros, Athea

'Meat for the Table': CBE 96 142 Tim McCoy, Gortmacross

'Stolen Butter': Kevin Danaher, *Irish Customs and Beliefs* (Mercier Press,
1964), p. 105

'Biddy Early's Message': NFCS 500:424. Martin Moyland, Ballyallinan
South. Collector: Agnes O'Grady. School: Duxtown, Rathkeale

'Biddy and the Butter': NFCS 528:284. Maureen Sheedy. Kilmallock
Convent School

'Anna Cliar and Biddy Early': NFCS 517:216-218. Mary Meaney,
Castlequarter. Collector: Máirtín S. Ó Maoldhomhnaigh, Fedamore

'Not All Can Be Saved': NFCS 510:106, 111, Cill Fhíonáin (B)

4

THE FOOL
MAKES GOOD

TADHG AND THE THIEVES IN THE WOOD

There was once a poor old widow who lived alone but for her son Tadhg. The boy was hardly a blessing to her, as he was a bit of a fool and known in the vicinity as Tadhg Saonta or 'Simple Tadhg'.

One year came that was worse than those before it, and if they had been poor, now things were dangerously close to penury. 'There is nothing for it, Tadhg, but you must go out into the world and find work. Otherwise we shall both surely starve.'

Tadhg set out the very next day. He walked all through the morning and through the afternoon. When the sky began to darken, he was walking through a wood, and saw a light in the distance. He thought he would make that his stop for the night. As he drew closer to the house he could hear the voices of men playing cards inside. Tadhg knocked at the door, and asked could he sleep there the night.

'Come on in, boy, and very welcome you are to share our humble abode,' said one of the men. They brought him in, drew up a chair for him by the fire, and gave him a bite to eat. They were kind to the boy because they thought he must have some money on him.

The men were a gang of thieves, who often waylaid travellers and stole their gold or jewels. The little house, hidden away well off the beaten track, was their headquarters, where they would meet up to plan their next robbery and share out the spoils of the last.

During the night, while Tadhg slept, the robbers searched his pockets and his bag, but found not one penny.

In the morning, they told Tadhg to be on his way, 'But be sure to call again when you have made your fortune and are on your way back home.'

Tadhg walked on all through the next day. He walked along a deep valley, and spied a little house by the side of a river. The door was open, and looking inside, Tadhg saw a white-haired fellow sitting by the fire. The old man called out to Tadhg, 'Come on in, lad and get a bite to eat'. Tadhg took the seat on the other side of the fire, and told his story.

'I have need of a strong young fellow like you to help with jobs about the place. You can stay here and work for me for three months. At the end of that time, I will give you your wages.'

So Tadhg stayed in the pleasant green valley and worked each day, rested at night, and ate whatever was put in front of him. When the three months had passed, the old man gave Tadhg a black hen.

'Is that my wages?' asked Tadhg. Never having got wages before, he did not know what to expect.

'It is,' said the old man. 'But listen to me, boy, this is no ordinary hen. She will lay you a golden egg every time you give her a handful of oats, if you ask her to and treat her well.'

Tadhg thanked the old man, picked up his bag, and with the black hen under his arm, he set off back along the road he had come.

He walked all day, and as night was coming, he remembered the invitation to call again to the house in the wood on his way home. He knocked on the door.

'Come in, boy,' called the robbers, expecting that he might have a purse of gold after three months of work in the world. When they saw the black hen, they laughed at Tadhg. 'Is that all you have to show for three months' work? What a fool you are!'

'Just wait till you see what she can do,' said Tadhg, taking a handful of oats and feeding the hen, saying, 'My little black hen, lay me a golden egg.'

When the hen laid her golden egg, Tadhg fed her again, and then again, and each time she laid another golden egg. Soon there was a pile of twenty golden eggs on the table.

'Well, now, that is a mighty hen you have there, my boy,' said the robber chief. 'You must be tired after walking all day. Why don't you go and sleep up in the loft? We will take care of your hen for the night.'

Tadhg was so grateful for the bed, that he fell asleep as soon as he laid down his head. While Tadhg slept, the robbers stole his hen and replaced it with one of their own.

In the morning, Tadhg picked up his bag, tucked the black hen under his arm and set off for home.

His mother saw him coming, and was at the gate to meet him. 'Why Tadhg, is that all you got paid in wages? A black hen?'

'Ah, mother, this is no ordinary hen. If you watch her a moment, she will lay us a golden egg.'

Tadhg gave the hen a handful of oats, but nothing happened. The hen gobbled up the oats, clucked happily, but there was no egg.

The woman raised her eyebrows, 'Oh Tadhg, what am I to do with you? Did you not learn any sense out there in the world?'

Tadhg slept that night in his own bed, and set out next morning, back to the house in the wood. He told the robbers that his hen would not lay. 'Ah now, that will be because she has got too fat. You must have been feeding her too often. Did you not know that fat hens will not lay an egg?'

Tadhg thought about the twenty golden eggs the hen had laid the night he stayed at the robbers' house. 'Oh, I see,' he said. 'I had better not feed her for a while then.'

Next day Tadhg made his way to the little house by the river in the glen. The old man welcomed him back, gave him jobs to do, a bed to sleep in, all the food he could eat, and promised him a decent wage when three months was done.

When three months had passed, the old man gave him a magic tablecloth. 'When you spread the cloth, it will be covered with food.'

Tadhg thanked the old man, picked up his bag, stuffed in the tablecloth, and set off back on the road home. He stopped that night at the robbers' house, and told them about his tablecloth. He spread the cloth on the table, saying 'Let there be food aplenty!' The robbers' eyes grew wide at the sight of the delicious food, and they all gathered round to share the feast.

While Tadhg slept, the robbers stole his magic tablecloth, and replaced it with one of their own.

When Tadhg reached home the next day, his mother was waiting for him at the gate. 'What have you to show for your three months' work, Tadhg?'

'Wait till you see this, mother!' said Tadhg, spreading the cloth on his mother's table, but nothing happened.

Tadhg's mother was so angry. She raised her eyebrows up to the heavens, 'Oh Tadhg, what am I to do with you at all? Did you not learn any sense out there in the world?'

Tadhg slept that night in his own bed and set out again next morning for the house in the glen. He worked another three months for the old man, and this time was rewarded with a magic blackthorn stick. 'Make sure that you stop for the night at the house in the wood. I think your friends will be greatly amused by what happens when you sing to the blackthorn stick!'

Tadhg set off for home, and stopped that night at the house in the wood.

'Welcome Tadhg,' said the robbers, 'and will you show us what you got as your wages this time?'

'Oh I will,' said Tadhg, and he sat down, brought out the black-thorn stick, and began to sing, 'Bring me my hen and bring me my cloth, my dear little blackthorn stick.'

The blackthorn stick set about beating the robbers all around the room, and it did not stop until they were black and blue. All that time Tadhg just kept on singing, until the robbers screamed for mercy and fetched his black hen and his magic tablecloth. 'Take them and go,' they yelled to Tadhg, 'but, for the name of God, call off the blackthorn stick!'

Tadhg stopped his singing then. He took up his hen under his arm, folded the cloth and put it in his sack, and with his blackthorn stick in his hand, he took his leave of his 'friends', and brought all of his wages home to his mother.

There was his mother waiting for him at the gate. When she saw the hen and the cloth and the stick, she smiled, and welcomed her boy back home. Maybe this time he had learned a bit of sense out there in the world! Tadhg and his mother lived there happily for the rest of their days.

Pat and the King's Gold

A long time ago there lived an old man and an old woman. They were happy together in most ways but one: they had no family to inherit their land and property. They did not own much: just 2 acres of land, a cow, two goats and a small store of money in coins.

Late one evening, as the old man was passing the churchyard on his way home from visiting a neighbour, he met an old woman. She greeted him warmly and asked him, 'Is there something that is bothering you? They say a trouble shared is a trouble halved, after all.'

'There is nothing much at all, but that I would like to have a son who would close my eyes when I am dead, and who might inherit my small bit of property when my wife and I are gone. But we are too old now for that to happen.'

'I think your wish will be granted,' said the old woman. 'Go home now and hear what news there is.'

When he reached home, his wife was as surprised as he to tell him that she was carrying a child. And within the year, to the astonishment of all the neighbours, a son was born. At that very moment, the old man was planting a tree in front of the house. When he heard that his son was born, his heart leapt with joy, but so hard that he fell down dead.

The wife was mad with grief, to have borne a new son and yet have no husband. She swore that she would never be satisfied until her son could uproot the tree that had been planted on his birthday – the day of her husband's death.

The child was strong and healthy, and she named him Pat. For seven years she fed and nourished him well, and on his seventh birthday he was a stocky fellow. She told him to uproot the tree, but he was not yet strong enough to do it. For another seven years his mother fed and nourished Pat. Then on his fourteenth birthday, she told him to go and pull up the tree. Still, Pat was not able to shift it. Another seven years she fed and nurtured her son, and when he was 21 years old, she sent him out to pull up the tree.

By this time, he had grown strong and he bent his knees and straightened his back, took hold of the tree and pulled. The earth shook for miles around as the soil began to loosen around the roots. On his second attempt the tree came clear of the ground.

'My dear mother,' said Pat, 'You cared for me so well these three times seven years, now it is my turn to do something for you. I will make myself a walking stick from this tree and journey into the world to seek my fortune.'

The next morning Pat set off with his walking stick, which was at least 20 feet long and weighed more than half a ton. He travelled on until he met the king.

'I am looking for work,' said Pat. 'Do you have a job that needs doing?'

'What kind of work can you do?' asked the king. 'What are you looking for? What is your trade?'

'I have no trade,' said Pat, 'but I can do any kind of work a man can do.'

'Very well,' said the King. 'I will make a bargain with you. If you will do everything that I ask of you for the next six months, I will reward you well. I will give you your own weight in gold, and my daughter in marriage. If you should fail, then you will lose your head. How does that sound to you?'

'It sounds a fair bargain to me,' said Pat.

'Good. Here is your first task: go into that barn and thresh my corn until your breakfast is ready.'

Pat went in the barn and took up the flail to begin threshing. But it was so small in his big hand, it was like a toy. Pat took up his walking stick and threshed with it instead. The whole barn was threshed in no time at all.

'Now, bring me two buckets of water from the lake below, and you will find your breakfast ready when you return,' ordered the king.

Pat brought two barrels and filled them with water from the lake. The king was amazed. He thought of many tasks for Pat to do and his kingdom was soon transformed with all the work of Pat's hands during those six months.

At last the king asked his wise counsellors to think of some task that Pat would not be able to do. He had not expected him to succeed thus far!

'You could order him to dry up the lake that lies before your house. While he is working on that, your men can crack his skull with a millstone!'

'Excellent idea,' said the king. 'That should do the trick.' And he called Pat to him and explained the new task. 'Oh and when you have the lake dried up, I promise I will give you a new hat,' he promised Pat.

'Very well,' said Pat, 'but where am I to put all the water?'

'Put it in the next valley.'

Pat dug a tunnel through the hill from the valley to the lake, and he sent the water along it. The lake was dry, but for a few last drops. While Pat was busy clearing the last drops of water, the king's men threw down the millstone. It landed right on the middle of Pat's head, with his head sticking through the hole in the centre. Pat thought that this was the new hat he had been promised, and thanked the king for it.

Now the king knew there was no task that Pat could not do. He must pay him his wages. He told Pat to sit on the scales to be weighed, but Pat would not remove his new 'hat'.

'My daughter is too young to marry you, but I will pay you your weight in gold as we agreed,' said the king.

He had not quite enough gold to meet the bargain, but Pat did not complain. He took the king's two sacks of gold and threw them over his shoulder. Then, with his walking stick in his hand, over the hills and valleys he made his way merrily home to his mother.

He built her a fine new house and the two lived there happily for the rest of their days.

SEAN NA SCUAB – MAYOR OF LIMERICK

A long time ago in Limerick city, all the important men of the city gathered together to elect a mayor. You'd think that might be easy enough with a vote, but somehow no two could agree on who should be the mayor. Some made colourful speeches in praise of their choice. Others were more direct and said more in fewer words about theirs. Whenever one spoke up with his suggestion, another would shout him down, and that's how it went on for days, seeing as they had no mayor to help them make the decision. They were getting nowhere, tempers were rising, and angry words grew into fighting in the street.

At last one of the gentlemen called out, 'Enough! Reason has failed us. We have not been able to choose a mayor ourselves, so let us try another way. Perhaps chance will make the decision for us! Here is my idea. Let us go home now and gather at Thomond Bridge, down by the castle, at first light tomorrow. I say we wait for the first man to cross the bridge from the Clare side in the morning and make him the mayor of Limerick!'

That set the gentlemen arguing again, but as there was no other suggestion, they decided to go ahead. Early next morning they met at Thomond Bridge.

Now, over on the Clare side of the river there was a poor fellow living in a rough little hut on the bog near Cratloe, along with his mother. His name was Sean, and he made a meagre living out of gathering heather to make brooms and chimney brushes. He'd sell these to the country people who lived around him, wandering from place to place with his ass and car piled high with brushes. Sean na Scuab, Sean of the brushes, they called him. Sean wasn't the smartest of men, but he was an honest one. One evening he had no luck in selling his brooms, even though he'd travelled far around the countryside. He was near the top of a hill, and had a good view of the city of Limerick in the distance. He scratched his head, straightened his hat and thought to himself, 'There must be a good number of folks living there in that town. I'll stop here the night, and at first light, I'll go to Limerick market and try to sell my brushes.' He told his ass what he was thinking and then settled himself down to sleep under the stars on the hillside.

Early next morning, Limerick's rich and important men were getting impatient. They were all standing at Thomond Bridge, ready to greet their new mayor, but no one had passed their way at all. But wait a minute, what was that in the distance? They saw a man sitting up on a cart loaded high with brushes and drawn by an ass.

'Good morning!' they greeted him. 'Who are you, my good man?'

'My name is Sean. At home they call me Sean na Scuab, for I make heather brushes and brooms. I am on my way to sell my goods at the market in Limerick.'

'Well, you are most welcome to Limerick, Sean na Scuab,' said the gentlemen. 'You can forget about the market for now, for you are going to be the mayor of Limerick for a year and a day.'

'I don't know anything about mayoring!' protested Sean, but the men led him to the mayor's palace. They helped him out of his ragged clothes, gave him a good scrub with soap and water, and dressed him in red velvet robes, trimmed with ermine. They placed a gold chain around his neck and a mace in his right hand and seated him in the mayor's throne of office. The bishop came and before all the city's important men, Sean swore his oath. Sean na Scuab was now mayor of Limerick!

The rich men asked the new mayor's advice about this and that. Sean, having no education at all, couldn't read so much as a single letter on a flour bag. But he was an honest man, and he gave his answers without guile or prejudice. The city's gentlemen were delighted to have someone to tell them what to do.

That night Sean slept on a feather mattress in a four-poster bed in the mayor's palace. 'Well now, this is the life,' thought Sean, 'I could get used to this!' Outside everyone was busy decorating the streets of Limerick for the mayor's parade the following day.

Meanwhile, back in Cratloe, Sean's mother was worried. Sean had not been home for two nights running. She thought some terrible thing must have happened to him. She went around asking if anyone had seen him. At last she heard from an old man on the road that Sean had gone to Limerick. 'Ah,' she thought, 'He must be out carousing in the city. I had better go and save him from himself.' She set off for Limerick to bring him home before he ruined himself.

When she crossed the bridge, there were crowds of people everywhere. 'Have you seen my son, Sean?' she asked everyone she passed, but no one seemed to hear her. She was so caught up looking for Sean that she hardly noticed the ribbons and bunting that bedecked the city streets. But when the band came marching along the street, she had to take notice, and leap quickly out of their way. Behind the band, the soldiers, in their dress uniforms, marched smartly along, followed by a golden coach drawn by six white horses. The crowds of people lining the streets waved flags and cheered as the new mayor passed by. She looked up at the gilded coach. The mayor, in his red robe with the ermine edging, a gold chain around his neck, smiled and waved to the cheering crowd. She looked again. The mayor's face looked familiar. That was her son, Sean!

She called up to him, 'Sean, Sean na Scuab! It is your mother here!' Sean saw her, but quickly looked away, as if he did not know her.

She ran up to the coach, to look him in the eye, and called out again, 'Sean na Scuab, I hardly knew you, all scrubbed up and dressed in finery! Do you not know me at all? It is your own mother.'

And Sean na Scuab, the mayor of Limerick, replied, 'How could I know you, woman, when I don't even know myself?'

SOURCES

'Tadhg and the Thieves': NFCS 491:89. Broadford, Rathluirc, County
   Limerick
'Pat and the King's Gold': NFCS 488:17-26. Michael O'Grady, Barangue,
   Carrickerry. Collector: John Dalton, Glenbawn, Carrickerry. Scoil an
   Chúrnánaigh, Newcastle West, County Limerick

5

TALES OF THE FIANNA

Finn MacCool and his band of warriors, the Fianna, spent many a day hunting in the hills of County Limerick.

They left their names and stories inscribed on the landscape: hills, peaks and townlands bear their names. The highest peak in the Ballyhoura Mountains is called Seefin, or Finn's seat. Before St Patrick visited the county, the hill of Ardpatrick (which was later named after him as 'Patrick's high place') was known as 'Tulach na Féinne' or the hill of the Fianna. The townland of Glenosheen or Gleann Oisín is said to be the spot where Finn's son Oisín fell from his horse when he returned to Ireland from Tír na nÓg.

THE LAST OF THE FIANNA

One day when Finn and the Fianna were hunting, they encountered a stunningly beautiful young woman riding a finely ornamented horse. Her long hair was golden and, with the sun behind her, she seemed to spread a radiance all around. The Fianna were surprised to meet so fair a maid so far from any sign of civilisation. She rode towards them and stretched out her graceful hand, introducing herself, 'Good morning to you, brave warriors of the Fianna. My name is Niamh Cinn Óir and my father is the King of Tír na nÓg, in the far west beyond the waves. In our kingdom, it is always summer, and no one ever grows old.'

Finn answered her, 'We are at your service, Niamh of the golden hair. Tell us how we can help you.'

'Some time ago I spied one of your knights and he stole my heart,' said Niamh. 'I love him and I cannot live without him. I have been searching for him all around the country.'

The Fianna looked around at each other, each one of them silently wishing that he might be the one she sought. Niamh looked directly at Finn as she said, 'It is your son, Oisín, whom I seek.'

Finn's heart sank. He loved his son Oisín dearly and he knew that if Oisín went to Tír na nÓg he would never see him again. But Oisín could hardly believe his luck, that such a beautiful woman wanted him above all others. He stepped forward willingly, and took Niamh's hand. 'I would be honoured to come with you to your country.'

When Finn and Oisín had embraced and said their farewells, Oisín leapt up on Niamh's horse. With a tinkling of the harness bells, the young couple rode off into the west.

Oisín lived happily with Niamh in Tír na nÓg for 300 years. Each day was filled with joy and pleasure, all around them was beautiful and they wanted for nothing. In all that time Oisín aged not one day: it truly was the land of the ever-young. From time to time Oisín felt homesick and longed to see the land of Ireland again.

Niamh tried to explain, 'My dear, your country will not be as it was when you left. Time travels differently here in Tír na nÓg. You have not aged, but 300 years have passed in Ireland. Your friends and family will be long gone. If you set foot in Ireland, you may not return here again.'

'I would not get lost, Niamh. Our good horse surely knows the way home.'

His longing was so strong that Niamh could not dissuade him. 'I cannot stop you, but I warn you: do not place a foot on the earth of Ireland. Stay on our horse, for while you do, you are still a part of Tír na nÓg. If you step on the land, you must stay there and will be lost to me forever! Swear to me you will not step on the land.'

Oisín agreed, and the two parted. He rode the white horse over the waves to the green land of Ireland. His heart was glad to see the hills and roads he knew so well. But he could find no trace of the forts and palaces of the Fianna and everything appeared so small and dull. Ireland was not how he remembered it. He stopped a group of travellers and asked them, 'Where will I find Finn MacCool?'

'You would need to look in his grave, for he has been dead nearly 300 years!' came the reply.

'But here, you look a strong young giant of a man. Could you lend us a hand? We are trying to move a stone that has fallen on our friend.'

Happy to help, Oisín leaned over in the saddle and stretched out a hand. With one hand he lifted the stone, and released the man trapped beneath it. But as he raised the stone, he lost his balance, and had to set down a foot to steady himself. Suddenly a great weariness came over him. As soon as his foot touched the earth, his hair first turned white and then fell away. His skin grew taut and dry, his eyesight faded. Too late, he remembered Niamh's warning and knew he would never see his love again. In the land beyond the waves, Niamh of the golden hair felt a tremor in her heart and wept. The white horse ran off, making its way back home to Tír na nÓg.

A crowd gathered around the ancient man who now lay helpless on the earth. 'Fetch Patrick!' somebody called. 'He will know how to help the poor old fellow.'

They brought a man in a plain brown robe, with a wooden staff in his hand. He dipped a crust of bread in water and raised it to Oisín's lips. 'Eat this, old man, and then we can talk,' said Patrick.

Oisín stayed with Patrick for three months. Every evening he told the saint stories of his adventures with the Fianna and Patrick recorded these in his book. Each day Patrick told Oisín stories of his god and of the changes that the land had seen. The two laughed and argued and became good friends. When Oisín, the last of the Fianna, lay dying, he asked St Patrick to baptise him into the new faith.

The Curse of the House of the Rowan Trees

A long time ago, Finn did battle with the King of Lochlainn. Having won the battle, Finn slew the king, but showed mercy and spared the king's young son, Midac Mac Lochlainn. Finn took Midac into his own home and he grew up within Finn's own household, where he was shown hospitality, given all that he might need, and a scholar's and a warrior's training. He was quick to learn, skilled with a spear and a sword, even if he was a surly child. Despite his prowess, no one warmed to the boy and he made few friends because he kept a sullen expression on his face at all times. When Midac reached adulthood and Finn could be free of his obligation to him, Finn offered him lands to build his own palace. Midac chose land at Kenry, near the Shannon and there he built his stronghold. It was a good choice: the river opened out here, there were islands and safe harbours. He gathered around him a band of young warriors, but for fourteen years he sent no invitation to Finn to visit him. Finn thought only that the boy needed time to settle and took no offence at his lack of gratitude. Midac secretly hated Finn for killing his kin and swore to one day take his revenge on his foster father.

Some years passed by and Finn and his men were once more hunting in the Limerick hills. They made camp on Knockfeerina, in the early evening and were preparing to eat. Suddenly they became aware of a young man in a scarlet cloak, striding towards them. He wore a sword and a helmet, and yet he spoke with the tutored voice of a bard.

'I saw a great army pass over these hills, whose riders had no horses, only plants and branches. They robbed all before them.'

'I believe it was an army of bees you saw,' said Finn, 'who stole sweet nectar from the flowers as they passed!'

'I saw a woman swifter than the swiftest horse. Her children are silver flashes, her bed is crystal.'

'I believe she is Bóand, the River Boyne, who is always in movement. Her children are the fishes who swim in her, the crystals her river bed.'

After he riddled some more, and Finn had answered all his verses, the young poet revealed himself as Midac Mac Lochlainn.

'You answered well, Finn. Now, come, I have a feast prepared for you and your men at the House of the Rowan Trees. I would repay the many kindnesses you showed to me in my youth.'

Finn, having wondered when he might at last be invited to Midac's fort, went willingly, despite his men's suspicions that it might be some kind of trap: the rowan tree was known as a tree of enchantment. But the rules of hospitality were strong in those days, and it would have been most rude to refuse the invitation.

Finn brought with him Goll Mac Mórna, Conán Maol and a few others. He left his son Oisín, with Diarmuid, Fiachna and several others behind to meet up with the rest of the hunting party. It was always a good idea to cover one's back, just in case it was indeed a trap.

Midac led the party to a fine house surrounded by strong walls. Around these was a ring of rowan trees, heavy with red berries. The gates opened, and armed men came to lead away the horses. Stewards brought Finn and his men into a bright warm hall. The walls were hung with fine tapestries, showing scenes of the hunt; the floors scattered with richly coloured woven rugs. Wooden pillars, intricately carved, supported the roof. Huge logs burned in the grate, the flames dancing high, flickering green and gold, and sending out a sweet scent of resins and herbs into the room. Long tables lined by comfortable couches, piled high with soft sheepskins and furs, were laid with shining dishes. Midac excused himself, leaving Finn alone with his men.

'This is a fine house, is it not?' said Finn, looking around. 'Who would have thought Midac to be such a generous host? Perhaps I misjudged the boy.'

The men muttered among themselves for a while, wondering when their host might return and the feasting begin. No servants came to feed the fire, nor to fill their goblets. The light from the hanging lamps began to grow dim.

As the lights grew dimmer and eventually died, Finn remarked, 'This is a strange feast, with no host here to entertain us.'

'Strange it is, all right,' said Goll, 'for that warm fire that greeted us with its sweet scent is nothing now but stinking black sticks, spitting out soot and reek!'

'And the fine hangings are gone from the walls, which are only rough planks now, with gaps for the rain and wind to come through!'

'And the soft fleeces on the fine benches. Now it feels to me more like I am sitting on the hard cold ground that is covered with snow!' cried Conán Maol, looking down and finding this was in fact the case. 'And I cannot move, but am stuck to the ground!'

The warriors struggled to rise, but found themselves quite unable to stir.

'I think this would be a wise moment to use your thumb, Finn,' said Conán, 'for I swear, I do not know how else we are to get out of this accursed place!'

Finn took his thumb – the thumb that had blistered when he was cooking the salmon of knowledge for his master Finnegas, when he was a boy; the thumb he had stuck in his mouth to relieve the burning pain; the thumb that had shown him all that would unfold! Now a grown man, and in need of wisdom, he stuck his thumb in his mouth and chewed on it like a baby.

Now he saw the full picture: how Midac Mac Lochlainn had entrapped them here, using the magic of the three kings of the Isles of Torrents. He saw that the enemies were assembling now to finish them off. He saw that they could not free themselves, but only be freed by help from without, by a scattering of the blood of those same three kings at the gates of the House of the Rowan Trees.

'Comrades, we need help from outside. Let us send out the Fianna's battle cry!'

Finn's men drummed with their hands on the hard earth, and they cried out a ferocious war cry.

Now some of the Fianna who were still close by heard the mournful cry and came running to the House of the Rowan Trees. They spoke to Finn through the gaps in the walls, and learned what enchantment was on them, and what they must do to break it. They swore they would defend their captive comrades, whatever the cost to themselves. They chose a ford that Midac's men must cross to reach the House of the Rowan Trees, and there they waited for Midac's assault.

One of Midac's men thought that he could steal away and kill Finn himself. Surely Midac would reward him for such a feat? He set off secretly for the House of the Rowan Trees, but was slain by Fiachna at the ford.

The Fianna were hard pressed yet they held the ford against Midac's army, the bodies of those slain piling up in the water and turning it red. A bloody battle it was, but then Diarmuid's spear struck Midac through the throat, and he brought his head to Finn at the House of the Rowan Trees. There he heard what must be done to save his comrades and returned to the ford.

The three kings of the Isles of Torrents came at last to the ford, and Dairmuid fought each one in single combat. The fighting was fierce and long, but at last Diarmuid won the heads of all three kings. While Fodla held off the rest of the enemy, Diarmuid scattered the blood of the three kings around the House of the Rowan Trees, and the curse was broken.

Finn and his men were now free to move, but still in a very weakened state. 'It is a night's rest we need now. By sunrise tomorrow we will be restored to our full strength.'

Diarmuid and Fodla held the ford throughout the night. Before first light, more warriors arrived to swell the enemy force, and all seemed doomed. These two brave warriors had given their best, but could they withstand another day's fighting?

However, with the sunrise came Finn and Goll and Conán Maol, with the cry of battle rising from their throats, and their strength returned to them. The battle continued until Oisín arrived, bringing the rest of the Fianna, and the victory was sure.

It was many years before anyone dared threaten the might of the Fianna again!

Sources

'The House of the Rowan Trees': *Lady Gregory, Gods and Fighting Men*, Part II Book VI: 'The House of the Quicken Trees'

6

Áine's Sacred
Landscape

*The old people used to say that 'the sky is widest above Lough Gur'.
Perhaps this is because when the sun shines over the water it gives an
impression of space. Or maybe it is that we get a sense of expansion in
that magical landscape, can breathe easily, feeling literally 'in-spired',
filled with spirit and light there.*

*When I first visited the great stone circle, the Lios, I was newly
in love and perhaps that coloured or enhanced my first impression.
However, the circle itself was impressively atmospheric, and still has
its own power to enchant. Amongst its stones, as if part of the circle,
there were ash trees growing, their grey bark gnarled and formed into
patterns like Celtic interlace. The stone circle is but one feature of an
extensive sacred landscape. There are several other stone circles, standing stones, avenues, cairns, dolmens, ancient habitation sites and caves
within the area.*

*Whilst working on this book, I returned to the Lios and the area around
Lough Gur, to remind myself of what it felt like here. To put myself back
into this landscape that I had visited so often at special times: seasonal
festivals like Bealtaine, Midsummer, Lughnasadh, and so on. I had come
here on many different occasions with drummers, with poets, with children,
with a wedding party. I had come here alone at times and met peace and
stillness; I had on occasions met witches, healers, dowsers, farmers, dancers,
tourists, people seeking answers, people who needed to talk. Other times
I met only bullocks, rain, mud and my own self-reflected from the lake*

surface. Perhaps that is how it had always been here. People gathered at those liminal times of the turning year. What has not changed is the power of the place.

I came first with an archaeologist's eyes, and a poet's soul, and my heart was blown open. I did not know its stories back then, but it became part of my story. When I returned, having meanwhile learned many of the stories that live here, it was as a storyteller, with ears attuned for the truth.

How Lough Gur Came to Be

There was a spring well in the area. It was a 'boiling well', meaning that it was an ever-flowing spring. There was a stone cover over the well and everyone knew that they must replace the cover after taking water from the spring. One day a young woman went for a bucket of water. She took off the lid, filled her pail, and in her hurry to get back home, she forgot to put the cap back on it. The water rose up from the spring like a fountain, and spread to cover the land all around. The force of the water carried the girl away and she was drowned in the lough.

An alternative story is that an old woman was passing water near a well in the area. St Patrick, who was making his way around the county back then, came passing by, and seeing the old woman called out a blessing to her, 'May God increase you!'

The old woman carried on with her business. All the while the water was rising around her, and in the end that was how the lake came to be there.

Áine: Dé Danann Goddess, Queen of the Munster Fairies

They say that Áine was queen of the Munster fairies. Her home is the hill of Cnoc Áine that rises by the village of Knockainy, between the town of Hospital and the Lios, the extensive stone circle in Grange townland. Cnoc Áine is said to be one of three fairy hills in County Limerick: Cnoc Áine (Knockainy); Cnoc Gréine (near Pallasgreen); and Cnoc Fírinne (Knockfeerina).

Áine is one of the oldest of the gods. She was/is a goddess of the *Tuatha Dé Danann*, and the land of Munster was her sacred ground. She oversaw the fertility and prosperity of the land and its inhabitants. *Tuatha Dé Danann* means 'the people of the goddess' Danu, and some scholars claim that Áine may be the same as Ana, Anu, or Danu. Perhaps she was the mother of this race of gifted craftspeople, seen as gods and later to become the *sidhe* or fairies. The sovereignty of Munster was hers to confer on any man who sought to rule there. It is easy to see Áine as the sun, the light that sparkles on the waters of Lough Gur, the enlivened air. Her name means 'delight, joy, radiance, harmony, truth, brightness'.

The wild herb meadowsweet is known as Áine's plant. Also known as 'queen of the meadow', meadowsweet has healing properties, containing in its leaves a substance that relieves headaches, inflammation and many other complaints. Its flowers are light and airy, and, as the name suggests, they fill the air with their scent in late summer, the time of harvest.

A great queen, at times Áine seems to be a young girl or an old woman. She is a lover, a rape survivor, a mermaid, mother of a poet, the woman who knits, the *cailleach*. She is a true goddess, and her presence can still be felt in the landscape, in the air, in the names given to landscape features.

She was spoken of as the 'best-hearted woman that ever lived', and people in the area spoke highly of her. At times she would disguise herself as an old woman to walk among the people. In the guise of a beggar woman, she wandered the roads. As night came on, she came to a little cabin where an old man and woman lived. With hardly enough to feed themselves, still they opened their humble home to her and shared what they had. They were surprised to find an unfamiliar sheep in their field next morning. While they kept the sheep, Áine's gift to them for their hospitality, all went well for them and they prospered. Their fortune changed when they sold the sheep at market and they became as poor as ever they had been.

Áine's father was Manannán Mac Lir, and her foster father the King Eogobal, and many familes claim to be her descendants. These include the O'Briens, O'Deas, and of course the Fitzgeralds, but that is another story (see p. 69, Gearóid Iarla).

AILILL OLLAM: AN UNFIT KING

Ailill was the King of Munster, way back in mythological times. It was at *Samhain*, Hallowe'en, when he encountered Áine who was playing sweet music on a lyre or harp, and, dazzled by her bright beauty, he wanted her. Ailill forced himself upon her. Áine was no passive victim, but fought back courageously against the rape. Disgusted by this assault, she managed to bite Ailill's ear, leaving it torn and bleeding.

Áine's response to rape had a deeper significance than purely self-defence. As sovereignty guardian, Áine could grant, or take away, the right to rule. Under the ancient laws, a king had to be unblemished and whole in himself. Now that he was disfigured by the damage to his ear, Ailill was no longer fit to be king. His shameful behaviour should perhaps have already proven him unworthy, but now there was a visible sign for all to see.

From then on he was known as Ailill Ollam, the one-eared.

As a result of the rape, Áine gave birth to a son, Eogan, who later became a king of Munster. From him the Eoganacht lineage claimed its descent.

THE HOUSEKEEPER'S CHAIR

There is an earthen mound and a large stone called Suidechán Bean Tíghe, or the Housekeeper's Chair, near the edge of the lake at Knockadoon. This was Áine's birthing chair where she laboured to give birth to her son. From here she also, as mother of the harvest, gave birth to the first sheaf of corn at the festival of *Lughnasadh* (late July/early August).

Anyone who dares to sit upon the stone will either be driven mad or be cured of their madness. Áine bestows her gifts of inspiration to the poet and artist, or she might draw them so far from themselves that they might never find their way back!

Áine could still be seen there, from time to time, as 'lady of the lake' or in the form of a mermaid. She would sit there combing her long hair with a golden comb, and when she was done, she'd set the comb aside and sleep.

There was a young herdsman who watched her, sitting on the mound as she combed her hair with a golden comb. When she had finished smoothing out the tangles, she laid herself down and slept. The herdsman saw this as a chance to steal away her comb. It was gold and would surely be worth something. As he sneaked up on the sleeping mermaid, she heard not a single step, but slept on soundly. He took the golden comb, but from that day on he had nothing but bad luck, one thing after another befalling him. It was not long after that he lay dying. He called out to his parents to take the golden comb and throw it back into the lake.

After his funeral, his mother and father walked sadly to the lake shore and cast the golden comb into the water. They turned and were walking homewards when they heard a splashing. Turning back, they saw a hand rise from the lake, holding aloft the golden comb.

Now the comb was returned to her, the mermaid let no further misfortune befall the herdsman's family.

She Who Knits the World's Green Cloth

Beneath the enchanted waters of Lough Gur, there grows an ancient and enormous tree, concealed beneath a green cloth. Beneath the green cloth a woman sits at the base of the tree. She is knitting with a green yarn the fabric of the world, and will continue to do this until the end of the world, or until the enchantment on the lake is broken. Once every seven years, when the waters of the lake recede, the tree and its covering are revealed.

One day, when the waters of the lake were low, there came a horseman riding by. Seeing the green cloth, so fine and beautiful, he snatched it up, revealing the knitting woman beneath it. She cried out to the waters of the lake:

Awake, awake, thou silent tide!
From the Dead Woman's land a horseman does ride,
From my head the green cloth snatching.

As she spoke, the waters of Lough Gur began to rise. The rider kicked his horse into action and raced off, but the waters came leaping and foaming behind him. Horse and rider were swept into the lake and were lost beneath its waves. The green cloth slowly drifted down through the water until it came to rest once more over the tree and the knitting woman.

Some say that had the cloth been stolen, the fertility of the land would have been destroyed.

In our own time, when soil and crop fertility are sorely threatened, not by horsemen riding by, but by man-made causes such

as artificial fertilisers, the death of bees, genetic manipulation and climate change, perhaps we should all be taking up our knitting needles and green yarn to help 'knit the world better'! Áine urges us to join her, to do what we can to recreate the green fabric of life.

Today there is a large stone called the *cloch a bhile*, which means the 'stone of the tree', not far from the great stone circle at Lough Gur.

CLOUGHAUNAINEY

There were flagstones forming a bridge across the Camoge River, near Knockainy. It was one of the oldest bridges in Ireland, as Áine was said to have carried the flagstones there in her silken apron and placed them in the river herself. The old bridge was destroyed and the flagstones removed in the 1930s to facilitate drainage works and the building of a new bridge. The men who blew it up said that they saw Áine Cliar appear before them, and that she told them the first man to walk on the new bridge would die.

It was the son of a man who was building the new bridge that was the first to walk on it and true enough he did die – but then, will that not come to us all one day?

ÁINE CLIAR AT MIDSUMMER

Áine Cliar, she is called in folk memory: Áine of the lights, Áine the beautiful. That memory was held brightly and honoured with gatherings on her hill, Cnoc Áine, in the heart of her sacred land-scape. At Midsummer's (St John's) Eve, the people carried *cliars* or torches made from bundles of dry straw attached to long poles to the top of Cnoc Áine, and later brought them, still burning, through their fields, to ensure Áine's blessing on their crops and cattle for the year ahead.

One Midsummer's Eve a group of girls delayed on the hilltop. They were no doubt enjoying the midsummer games and the view from their vantage point, where they could watch the lights being carried down the hill and through the fields. They were singing and dancing when Áine herself appeared among them, bright as the sun. Áine very politely asked them to leave, saying she was delighted they had come to her hill that night, but would they now go home. Áine's otherworldly friends were waiting, for it was now time for their own celebrations. Áine held up her ring, so that the girls could peep through it and see the fairy host gathered on the hill. Having no wish to displease Áine, the girls left at once, but they did not forget that very special midsummer meeting.

MOONLIGHT AND MUSIC

As the full moon approached, people would bring their sick to the lake shore to moon-bathe, so that the moonlight would shine brightly on them near the water. The old people called the night 'all heal'. If a sick person was not better by the eighth or ninth day of the moon, they would then hear the *ceol sidhe* (fairy music), which Áine, as the spirit of Lough Gur, would sing or play to comfort the dying. The sick person would fall asleep to the comforting 'whispering song of sleep' which Áine's brother Fer Fí would play on his harp.

Fer Fí was said to be a good-natured red-haired dwarf, whose home was in Knockfennell. He played a harp with three strings, and had only three melodies: *goltraighe*, the sad and lamenting music; *geantraighe*, the music of joy and laughter; and *suantraighe*, the music of magical sleep, from which mortals might never awaken. To hear the laughing music was a sign of sure recovery, while hearing the lamentation meant a cure was unlikely.

Sean O'Hea and the Woman in the White Dress

Sean O'Hea was a piper, and there was hardly a dance tune that he could not play. Whenever he played, the people present could not control their feet. First they would be tapping at the ground, but it wouldn't be long before their legs carried them up and dancing despite themselves.

Sean and his wife Judy lived in a small cottage at the foot of the hill of Knockadoon, overlooking Lough Gur. Whenever there was a wedding, or a christening, or any other kind of gathering, a message would come asking Sean to play his pipes. Sean was always rewarded well for his playing, so himself and his wife were never short of money, but lived comfortably enough in their cosy little home.

One evening in late summer Sean was out walking around Knockadoon, checking on the cattle. He was taking his ease, enjoying the mild August evening, the gentle breeze, the light reflecting from the lake, and the beautiful scenery all around him. All was well in his world, with nothing to disturb him. When he heard a voice behind him, he turned, and there was a lovely young woman all dressed in white.

'Good evening to you, Sean O'Hea,' she said in a soft, sweet voice that sounded to Sean the way honey tastes.

'And good evening to you too, miss,' said Sean. 'Can I help you? Have you lost your way? Are you looking for somewhere?'

'It is yourself, Sean, I was looking for. I have come to fetch you to play your pipes at a ball tonight.'

'Aha, is that so?' said Sean.

'You can be sure there will be a generous reward if you choose to come with me.'

'Is it far I'd have to go?' asked Sean. 'Only my wife Judy would be mad with me if I am away for too long. Sure, she would be so cross she would not smile at me for seven days or more!'

'It is not so far, Sean,' said the lady, 'but perhaps it is best that you go and ask your good wife first before you come with me. I will wait here for your return.'

Sean made his way home and told Judy about the lady in white. Judy was not keen and tried to dissuade him from going.

'I do not think you should go with this stranger, Sean. Let me tell you, I had a strange dream this morning and it has left me afraid that something bad will happen,' said Judy. 'I dreamed I was making my way home from old Nellie's, having fetched some starch, and didn't the starch turn as yellow as gold? And on the road home, there was a fine lady in a carriage throwing up two gold balls with one hand and catching them in the other. All the time she was looking down at me with a mocking sneer on her face. I was so afraid that I woke shaking and in a fever. I don't know what it means, Sean, but it surely was a warning.'

'Away with you, Judy!' said Sean. 'You made your tea too hot and too strong last night. It was only a dream, and there is no harm in that. She promised she'd pay me well. I must go now, for the lady will be getting impatient waiting for me so long.'

What Sean did not know was that the lady in the white gown was none other than Áine, the queen of the Munster fairies, and the ball was to be in the fairy palace of Knockfennel.

Saying goodbye to Judy, Sean tucked his pipes under his arm and made his way back to the spot where the lady in white was now sitting in a magnificent carriage, drawn by two fine grey horses. She opened the carriage door and bade Sean to join her inside. When he had climbed in and settled beside her, the horses trotted off along the road.

As the carriage wound its way along the narrow lanes, not one word was spoken between them. Sean did not know what he could have said to such a fine lady, and she herself just sat and smiled, with a faraway look in her eyes. Soon they were travelling along wide avenues lined with tall trees heavy with fruits, and the perfume of sweet scented roses wafted in the air. At last they stopped before a grand mansion. The doors were open and Sean was led into to the ballroom.

What a sight it was! Gentlemen in frock coats embellished with golden braids bowed to him. Ladies in wide satin gowns with low necklines curtseyed before him. Tall mirrors stretched from floor to ceiling and the lights of a hundred golden candelabras were reflected there.

A tall glass full of a golden drink was brought for Sean, and he downed it in one. It was an unfamiliar taste, fiery but sweet. 'Will you make sure ye have a good measure of the "cratur" for me in the morning before I go home!' he said. Then he sat himself down in a gilded chair and made ready to play his pipes.

That whole company was up and dancing straight away. The small, the tall, the fat, the thin, the strange and the beautiful, every one of them was on their feet. Sean played tune after tune, the whole night through, without a rest. His eyes were on the lovely young women as they whirled and reeled around the room, a fine colour in their cheeks. But now and then he had the strange thought, while he was playing, that he saw shoals of fish gazing in at him through the large windows of the ballroom. He wondered then, perhaps he was not in fact just some miles from home along the road, but instead in the palace of Gearóid Iarla, beneath the enchanted lake? But never mind that, still he played on and on, and all the good folk danced, and laughed and never took a rest the whole night long.

At last his hostess brought Sean his glass of the 'cratur'. He laid down his pipes, and took his drink. As soon as the music stopped, the dancers, exhausted, retired to their beds. But before they disappeared, each of the dancers placed a golden guinea into Sean's hat.

The lady in white came to Sean then, and handed him a small purse. 'It is a *sparán an tsallainn*, a bag of salt, that will never be found empty,' she explained. 'Thank you for your playing, Sean O'Hea. I told you there would be a grand reward.'

Sean thanked her, and then, exhausted himself from the whole night's piping, he fell into a deep sleep.

When Sean awoke, the sun was already high in the sky. He was cold and stiff and, rolling over, he found he was lying out on the damp ground. He sat up, rubbed his eyes, and looked around. Where was he but up on the top of the Suidechán Bean Tíghe, and all his golden coins were nothing but dry gold-and-copper leaves!

He unfastened the strings and opened up the purse. Inside, he found that the lady in the white dress had kept her word, and the purse was still full of salt. At least Judy would be grateful for that, for salt, after all, is the one thing that makes everything taste good.

Sean had been known all around as a piper, but after that August night, he had another claim to fame. Now he had a fine tale to tell by the fireside of a winter's evening.

Sources

'She Who Knits': *Mythic Ireland*, Michael Dames quoting 'an old woman from Askeaton, 24 April, 1879'

'Moonlight and Music': NFC 516:5c, 216, 1938

'Sean O'Hea and the Woman in White': NFCS 517:8. Owen Bresnan, Lough Gur, Limerick. Ballinard (B) School

7

GEARÓID IARLA

Maurice, the Earl of Desmond, was a Norman knight whose castle was near Lough Gur. Many stories are told in the area of his son, Gearóid Iarla or Earl Garret, a half-human, half-fairy warrior-enchanter, who rises from the lake every seven years on a white horse with silver shoes.

The Desmond earls were the kind of settlers who had a great respect for the native culture, and became 'more Irish than the Irish' through their love of Irish language, music and poetry.

One day as he walked by the shore of Lough Gur, Maurice, the first Earl of Desmond, saw a swan gliding on its calm surface. When the swan came to the shore, it took on human form, removing a white cloak and laying it on a rock by the water's edge. A stunningly beautiful young woman, tall and slim, and glowing with life and light, stepped into the water to bathe. From behind a bush he admired her long legs, the curve of her hip, the roundness of her belly, her upturned breasts, the gentle smile on her lips. Maurice was overwhelmed by her beauty, but more than that, never before had he seen such grace. His heart leapt in his breast: he knew this woman must be his love.

It was none but Áine, the beautiful *Dé Danann* goddess whose name speaks of joy and delight. Bright Áine whose beauty inspires love and desire. Áine who had power to confer sovereignty of the Munster lands upon those she saw fit. As she walked to the shore, drops of water sparkling with rainbow light fell from her body. When she picked up her golden comb and began untangling her long fair hair, Maurice quietly lifted her white cloak from the rock.

With this in his possession, Áine would be in his power: she would be his to love.

Áine turned her face towards the earl, and her smile was warm and radiant as the sun, offering Maurice an invitation to delight. She went with him willingly and the pair lay together, sharing pleasures the whole day long by the lake shore.

As evening came they rested and Áine told Maurice that she would bear him a son. 'You will not see me again until I bring your son to your castle, nine months from this day.' Wrapping herself in her swansdown cloak, Áine was gone. Maurice looked everywhere: along the shore, behind bushes, on the water, but there was no sign of the beautiful Áine who had so enchanted him.

True to her word, Áine remained hidden from the earl throughout her pregnancy. Where she spent her days as her belly swelled, he did not know. He had heard it said that Áine dwelt in a fairy palace within the hill named after her, Cnoc Áine; that she was ever-young. The people held fairs and dances below Áine's hill, and each three months they still marked festivals from the old times when the ancients had worshipped the sun. Yet faithful as the sun itself, Áine appeared at the castle door nine months later, and in her arms was a sleeping child wrapped in a knitted blanket.

'Here is your son,' she told the earl, handing the infant into his arms. The earl's face opened into a broad smile as the baby grasped his finger.

'Swear to me you will take care of him,' she beseeched the earl.

He agreed, 'He is my son and my heir, and as precious to me as the air I breathe. I will. Of course I will.'

Áine continued, 'Get him a nurse for his early years, and as he grows ensure he has a good education, as befits a gentleman.'

He agreed that nothing less would do for the son of an earl.

'There is one thing more,' said Áine. 'I lay this on you as a *geis* that you dare not break. I warn you, do not show surprise at anything he does, no matter how extraordinary it is.'

'I hear your warning, Áine, and I will do as you say. I swear,' said Maurice, thinking, his mother is certainly an uncommon woman, so perhaps I should expect astounding things of the boy!

'His name is Gearóid and he will be remembered as Gearóid Iarla,' she said, then turned to go. Leaving her child in the earl's care, Áine once more vanished from human sight.

The days and years of Gearóid Iarla's childhood and youth passed without incident. He might have fallen from a horse landing in a bed of nettles, or been clobbered in a wrestling match, but these were fairly ordinary things that might befall any young man. He was a willing pupil and quickly learned all that his tutors could teach him. He became fluent in several languages, Irish, French, Latin, Greek; gained proficiency in mathematics; he read ancient texts, and wrote with a careful and skilled hand; he learned the arts of poetry and music and more besides. He learned the skills of horsemanship and sword-fighting, falconry and hunting. He learned how to make fire in the woods; how to make tools and weapons from a branch; how to defend himself with his bare hands; how to follow tracks and recognise the calls of wild creatures. He learned to dance and to paint, and some say he learned the art of magic too.

When Gearóid grew to manhood, he was a fine-looking man: dark, handsome, tall and strong, intelligent, quick-thinking and entertaining – quite the young earl! His father was proud of him and his accomplishments.

One evening the earl held a ball at his castle. The smartest of ladies and gentlemen were in attendance. For the first while Gearóid Iarla entertained the ladies with his poetry and his wit. All were charmed by his attention, his rich and mellow voice, his sensitivity. Next, he debated with the gentlemen on the politics of the day. All agreed that his opinions were well reasoned, his words convincing and his argument hard to resist.

When the music struck up for dancing, everyone was on their feet. Men, women, all ages and sizes, threw themselves enthusiastically into the dance. One young woman stood out of the crowd. She wore an elegant gown of green silk, held herself tall and pointed her toe with great delicacy. Each of her gestures was an example of such grace that all the other women felt put to shame. She stood up for every single dance, when others might have stopped to catch their breath. And although she seemed familiar, no one quite knew who she was. The young earl took her as a dancing partner and matched her every step.

When the dancing abated, the young woman entertained the party with feats of gymnastics, leaping the length of the long table, tumbling and turning in the air. When the cheering and applause died down, she turned to Gearóid Iarla and challenged him to perform a similar feat.

'That was quite a spectacle, young lady, but I am sure that my son can match it. Go on, my boy, and show us what you can do!'

Gearóid leapt onto the table and somersaulted his way along its length. 'Bravo!' called out the crowd, greatly impressed by his agility.

'You think that was impressive, well, wait till you see this!' called the young earl, taking a short run and then leaping straight into a bottle, and out again.

The entire room gasped with astonishment, including the old earl. He was so astounded by this feat that he called out to his son, 'Well done, son. I never thought you could do something like that, my boy. That was such a surprise! I am truly amazed!'

As soon as he heard himself saying those words, the earl regretted it.

'Oh, father! Do you not remember? My mother warned you never to show surprise at anything I do. You broke your word, and now you have forced me to leave you.'

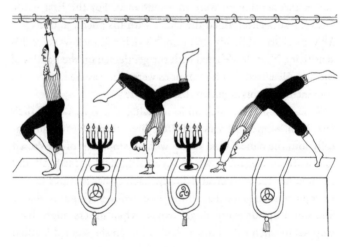

With those words, Gearóid Iarla left the hall. His shocked father and his guests followed him a little way. They watched the young earl stride down towards the Camoge River and step into the water. At once he lost his human form, and swam away in the shape of a goose.

Lough Gur and its environs are now a wild-fowl sanctuary, and geese are known to nest on Garret Island. Perhaps one of these is the young earl himself in bird guise.

SEVEN-YEAR CYCLE

After leaving his father's house, Gearóid Iarla took up residence in a palace beneath Lough Gur, the enchanted lake. There he had every comfort and all he might desire. Once every seven years, on Midsummer's Eve, he leaves his palace and is seen in the land of men. He rises from the water on a white horse shod with silver shoes, and leads his cavalcade of knights around Lough Gur. They say that anyone who sees him will die within the year.

The enchantment on him means that Gearóid Iarla cannot speak to anyone as he rides the land, but should someone speak to him first, then the spell would be broken and his voice restored.

It was high summertime and the days were long, the air was warm, and the light still good enough to see by. A blacksmith living near Lough Gur was working late into the night, when he heard hoof-beats approaching. He turned to see who was passing so late at night. Who should he see but Gearóid Iarla on his white horse, followed by his party of knights. Gearóid Iarla, unable to speak, pointed to his horse's shoe, wanting him to shoe the creature. The blacksmith, knowing the enchantment on the earl, would not speak to him, nor shoe his horse. The earl, in his frustration and rage, struck out at the blacksmith and disappeared into the night.

On another occasion, a man came into the forge near Lough Gur one evening and found a well-dressed gentleman there before him, with a white horse needing shoeing. 'Will you put a pair of shoes on my horse, my fine man?' the gentleman asked. The smith shod the horse, while the gentleman watched in silence. When it was done, he asked the man, 'Now will you lead my horse home for me? I will pay in silver for your trouble, but I cannot pay you until I am back home.' When the man agreed, the gentleman showed him a path leading out to the island in the lake.

When the smith reached the big house, the gentleman warmly welcomed him in. A servant brought him a suit of fine clothes to wear, and shoes with silver buckles. Once changed into this more suitable attire, the man was brought to the table and treated to a four-course meal. Everything around him was a delight to the senses. The furniture was elegant, yet comfortable; the walls richly coloured and hung with paintings of beautiful land-scapes; the tablecloth of the finest linen; there were china plates, and cutlery that balanced very well in his hand; the flowers in crystal vases filled the room with sweet aromas. After they had eaten, the gentleman thanked him for his work and gave him a purse full of silver. As it was now late, the gentleman led him to a room where a bed was prepared for him.

He slept so well in that warm, soft feather bed, but when he awoke next morning, he found himself lying on hard ground, with only his own old coat for a blanket. He saw that he was up on the side of Knockfennel Hill, looking down over the lake below. And what of the purse of silver, was it gone too? He checked in his pocket, but all he found there was a handful of leaves.

The Sleeping Warriors

Some say that Gearóid Iarla lies sleeping in a cave below Knockadoon, awaiting a wake-up call, when he will arise, take up his sword and, with his company of warrior knights, lead all Ireland to freedom.

A man was out walking one evening on the far shore of the lake, when he spotted a light on the hillside. Following the light, he came to a cave, partly concealed by briars and bushes. Pushing these

aside, he entered a passage and made his way deeper into the hill.
The passage opened up into a high-vaulted chamber. In the poor
light, he saw a party of warriors and horses on the cavern floor.
Scattered here and there lay helmets, spears, suits of mail and
weapons. Not far from where he stood, just beyond his reach, there
was a sword, its scabbard decorated with scrolls and gems, the hilt
gilded. It was a magnificent work of art, and it must have lain there
hidden and unhandled for hundreds of years. How he longed to
hold that silver sword in his hand! He stretched out towards the hilt
and slowly began to draw the sword from its scabbard. It was not an
easy task. It was stiff, and grated as he pulled, as if the sword did not
wish to leave its sleeping place. It must be rusted stuck, he thought.
Suddenly a horrible shrieking filled the air as the sword cried out to
its true owner, and the man dropped it as if it was a burning iron.
Warriors turned in their sleep and began to stretch, rubbing their
eyes. Their chief reached out his right hand for the sword, calling,
'Has the time come? Is it time for us to rise?'

While he still had his wits, the man called out, 'No, it is not
time yet! You must sleep a little longer, good knight,' and ran from
the cave out into the dark hillside. Nearly driven mad with fright,
he shook and shivered all the way home.

The party of knights rolled over and fell back into their dreams.
As no one since that night has found the entrance to the cave, they
will be sleeping yet, still awaiting their moment to rise and fight
for their country.

SOURCE

Michael Dames, *Mythic Ireland* (Thames & Hudson, London, 1992), pp.
  73–112

8

DONN OF
KNOCKFEERINA

*Knockfeerina, or Cnoc Fírinne, is one of the three fairy hills of
County Limerick, the others being Cnoc Áine and Cnoc Gréine near
Pallasgreen. Cnoc Áine and Cnoc Gréine are the residences of Áine
and Gréine respectively, while Knockfeerina is the fairy hill of Donn
Fírinne. Áine and Gréine may be two aspects of the one goddess: Áine
the light bright face of the summer sun; Gréine the darker, winter sun,
while Donn is an ancient Irish god of death and fertility.*

*When the Milesians, a race of ordinary mortal men and women,
came to Ireland, possibly from Spain, there was initially some con-
flict and competition with the existing inhabitants of the island,
the* Tuatha Dé Danann, *but in the end an agreement was reached
between the two races. The* Tuatha Dé Danann *took up residence
within the earth, in the hollow hills, as the Sidhe, the shining ones.
Over time they seemed to shrink in people's imaginations, and were
thought of as small fairy folk, the Good People.*

Donn Fírinne's fairy palace at Knockfeerina is just a few miles
from Ballingarry. It is one of the highest hills in the area, and its
summit provides a fantastic view over the broad plain of County
Limerick all around. People used to gather on Knockfeerina on
the eve of *Lughnasadh* in late summer to celebrate the harvest
with a bonfire and dancing. Girls brought flowers and fruit
as gifts for the fairy folk, in thanks for an abundant harvest.

The fertility of the land and prosperity of the people was a concern of the fairy folk, or before them, the gods. A shifting dynamic played out throughout the year. So, at *Lughnasadh* time, Donn and his fairy host would fight or play hurling with Áine's fairy host from Cnoc Áine. They would chase each other along the roads and fields between the two hills. Whichever fairy hill won the contest would claim the best of the potato harvest for their people that year.

Lios na bhFian or 'The Fort of the Fianna' lies on a part of the hill known as the Strickeens. This large fort may be the place where Finn MacCool and his men were tricked in the story of 'The House of the Rowan Trees'.

Donn Fírinne could gather mist and storm clouds about himself up on his hilltop. If you were to watch the hill in the morning, you could tell whether the day would be fine or wet, depending on whether the summit was clear or concealed by clouds. Thunder and lightning meant that Donn was out riding his white horse that night. The people would say, 'There goes Donn, galloping in the clouds tonight!' Or, 'I saw Donn in the clouds last night, so I knew it would be bad today.' Because it was usually a reliable weather forecaster, they called Knockfeerina 'the hill of truth'.

Donn Fírinne had his home in a deep hole, Poll na Bruinne, on the top of the hill. No one could say how deep it was; they said it was unfathomable. One fellow lay on his stomach at the side of the opening and dropped down a stone. He must have had a scientific bent, for he meant to determine just how deep it was from listening for how long it would take the stone to splash in the water, or hit rock below. Anyway he threw in his stone, and he waited, and waited, but he never did hear it clattering below. Instead, after a good few minutes, what should come flying back out of the hole in the hillside but his own cast stone. It hit him full in the face and left him with a broken and bloody nose. The fairies down below inside the hill were mad with him for throwing stones at them, so they threw it back to teach him a lesson.

A surveyor who sent down a plumb line into Poll na Bruinne felt someone below catch and tug at his line. The next thing he knew he was unable to let go of it, and so was pulled down into the hole. He was never seen again.

Donn would often ride the roads at night, or even fly through the air on his white horse. Those who met an unknown horseman on a dark road at night would cross themselves and say a prayer, just in case this was Donn bringing a death warning.

Perhaps Donn's mood changed with the weather, for on other occasions he was much more hospitable. Despite his association with darkness and death, Donn was often kind and friendly to those he met. He once gave the gift of sweet music to a harper, but withdrew it when the harper abused the gift to feed his own greed.

Once Donn invited a farmer, known for his good husbandry, into his great hall within the hill. The farmer was greatly impressed with Donn's palace, and Donn, pleased with his praise, allowed the farmer to take back home with him to the land of mortal men a brother and sister long thought to have died.

Donn Fírinne's Breakfast

Four men went out to dig up potatoes one day below Knockfeerina. One of the men was always out to make the others laugh: it passed the time and took the sting out of back-breaking work, after all. This time he joked, saying, 'I hear that Donn is a fine little fellow, generous and kind. I wonder, would he give us our breakfast since we are here below his house?'

'You should be careful what you say,' said another of the party, who had a superstitious nature and feared the anger of the fairy king. 'Donn will not be pleased to be mocked.'

Suddenly there was a lovely young woman standing before them. She laid out a white linen cloth on the grass, and set that with plates and cups, bread, butter and cheese and a pot of tea for four. 'Donn has provided some refreshments for those working hard below his hill. Will you come and eat your breakfast, gentlemen?' she asked them.

The men sat down and ate the delicious food, all except for the one who had asked for it.

'Will you not eat? After all, you are the one who called for it. It will do you no harm to eat Donn's food,' she said, smiling. But he would not touch it, not even a single bite.

The men got on with the work, and finished in good time. Nothing ill befell them, but the man who did not eat Donn Fírinne's picnic took ill that night and did not rise the next day.

THE FAIRY STOCKING

There was a young woman in the area who was always knitting. One day she sat near the entrance to one of the fairy caves at Knockfeerina. Her name was Kilbridge and she was known for her knitting, always busy with her needles and wool. As she worked this day, her ball of wool fell from her lap and disappeared, rolling down into the cave. She carried on knitting, but when she pulled on the yarn, didn't someone below in the cave pull back? She pulled on her yarn again, harder this time, and what came up from the cave was a whole knitted stocking? One half of it knitted in white, and the other half in red!

The only wool they had for knitting stockings in those days was white, so where had the red wool come from?

She kept that stocking carefully, and it became known as the fairy stocking, and she was called 'the knitting woman of Knockfeerina'. They said the fairy stocking was a cure for pains in the knees or other joints, and that anyone who put it on or rubbed their aching joints with it would find some relief and all thanks to the fairy knitter of Knockfeerina.

TOM THE PIPER OF KNOCKFEERINA

There was a poor farmer by name of Tom McKinney who lived near Knockfeerina long ago. Tom had had a run of bad luck, and now most of his cattle had fallen sick and died. He had no money and no idea of what he could do to get by in such hard times. The rent was due and he had a wife and child to feed.

Tom was a piper and his set of bagpipes was one of the few possessions he still had. He set to cleaning and polishing them one day, thinking maybe he could play his pipes in the nearby town and see if he might make a little money that way. He set off for town good and early next morning, hoping none of his neighbours would see him.

As he was passing a furze bush, who should step out from behind it but Donn Fírinne, the king of the Munster fairies!

'I see you are a piper, Tom McKinney. Will you play a tune for me?'

'I am sorry, sir,' said Tom, 'but my fingers are too cold for playing this early in the day.' And that was true, for it was a frosty morning.

Donn Fírinne reached out and took Tom's hands in his. From that moment on Tom played the pipes as if he'd been born to it. Every tune that came from his pipes was like a charm that could make you weep, or smile or laugh, or set to dancing, unable to stop.

'Now Tom, you take this bag of gold and take yourself off home. But tell me, will you come and play your pipes for me tomorrow night? Tell not one soul where you are going, but come just after the sun goes down. I will meet you here by this furze bush.'

Tom agreed, went home, and he handed the bag of gold to his wife, whose eyes lit up at the sight.

That evening, after his dinner, Tom told his wife he was going out to meet a friend, which in a way was not a lie. He made his way to the furze bush, and there was Donn Fírinne waiting for him on a big white horse, along with a party of eighty horsemen. They cheered and greeted him warmly and told him they were away to Clare to kidnap a lovely lady, and needed him to open the castle gates for them. Only a mortal man could do it. They warned him that he must keep his mouth shut and speak not one word until they brought him back again. Now that was a tough bargain, for Tom was a great talker, who was always full of questions and curiosity. Although the fairy host were on great war horses, they led Tom to an old plough horse, fitted out with a saddle and bridle. He climbed onto its back, and suddenly they were off! Rising into the night sky, they flew over the hedges and ditches, and straight across the Shannon. Tom forgot his silence for a moment, calling 'Good on ye, my old plough horse!'

No sooner spoken, than his sad old horse was stuck in the mud flats of the Shannon shore. Now Tom had to make his way back round by Sixmilebridge. Tom was sorry he had spoken. Would Donn Fírinne be angry with him? As he passed the furze bush, there was Donn Fírinne waiting for him with a bag of gold, and laughing about his mistake. All was forgiven, forgotten. But would Tom come again the following evening?

The next night, Tom was given a fine horse to ride so he could keep up with the others. This time Tom was to play his pipes outside the castle, to charm the guards with his music, while the fairy host stole away the lovely lady. Steal her away they did, although it did seem she was quite willing to be stolen. They brought her to Knockfeerina, where she was crowned queen of the fairies. Tom played again, all the dance tunes he knew and many he didn't even know he knew, and the whole fairy host were dancing and having the wildest of times. Donn Fírinne then insisted that Tom must stay a year and a day and play for him every night. Tom agreed to this. The days flew by, so that Tom felt it was just the one day he had spent there on the fairy hill. 'Haha!' said Donn Fírinne. 'You have been here a year, and all who knew you think you must be dead. A man who looks like you was found dead in a ditch around the same time you came away with us and now your wife is married to another man.'

That was quite a shock for Tom. What should he do now – go home or stay on the fairy hill? If his wife thought he was dead, dare he return and upset her? Would it be better if he stayed away?

Don Fírinne gave him another bag of gold and a gentle push in the direction of home. He said Tom should first visit his landlord, who was about to evict his family.

The landlord's face turned white when he saw Tom approach. 'Jaysus, I thought you were dead, man!'

'Well, dead or alive, we must still pay our debts,' said Tom, handing over what was owed on the rent.

The landlord, still in a state of shock, wrote out a receipt saying that no further rent was due, and that Tom's family could stay there forever without paying another penny.

Tom made his way home then, laughing as he met the neighbours and they ran from him. Outside the door, he met his own son and the boy ran for his mother. She came out to greet him, and welcome him home.

And her new husband? Well he wasn't really a husband at all, was he? Sure, the priest saw that all was sorted out and the man left quietly enough, now that Tom was home again and had his feet back under his own table.

SOURCES

'Donn Fírinne's Breakfast': NFCS 525:102 Mrs Mary Kirby, Croom, County Limerick. Ballymartin School, Croom, County Limerick

'The Fairy Stocking': NFCS 528:321. Patrick Kelly, Kilmallock. Kilmallock Convent School

'Tom the Piper': NFCS 528:327. Patrick Kelly, Kilmallock. Collector: Helen Mitchell. Kilmallock Convent School

Maire MacNeill, *The Festival of Lughnasadh* (Oxford University Press, 1962), pp 201–205

9

DREAMS

A GOLDEN KEY

There was an old man living around Knockpatrick who had a memorable dream. In the dream, he was ploughing a field, and he spotted something shining in a briar bush. When he stopped what he was doing and went to see what it was, he found a little golden key tied to the bush. At the same moment he heard a voice saying, 'If you dig down beneath that briar bush, you will find a box of gold coins.'

When he woke up, he did not bother to puzzle over his dream. He just got up, had his breakfast and went out to get on with his work. The next day he was ploughing a field when he noticed a little golden key fastened to a briar bush that had taken root in the earth. The key was pointing downwards towards the root of the bush. Suddenly he remembered the dream, and he knew there was gold hidden beneath this spot. Oh yes, he would like to be rich, but at the same time, he wondered if this was a trick the fairies were playing on him. He was a superstitious man, and finding the golden key had made him very anxious. No, he would not tempt fate, he would not dig for the gold.

He took the little key from the bush and put it in his pocket, and carried on ploughing the field. A few days later he was not feeling too well, and took to his bed. When his neighbours came to see if they could help him, he told them about his dream of the golden key and the treasure buried beneath the briar bush. 'Sure, you

don't need to be bothering about dreams. They are
not worth thinking about,' said the neighbours.
But when the old man showed them the golden
key he kept beneath his pillow, it was another story.

The neighbours said they would dig for the
gold, 'Tell us, where is the briar bush?'

The old man could not remember exactly where
it had been. When he was well again, he went
back to the field, but could not find the briar
bush. He still had the key, but the gold
beneath the briar bush remained a secret,
and may still be there to this day.

HIDDEN TREASURE

In Askeaton there lived a man called Pat O'Donnell. He was a
bachelor who had a great love of money. They say he used to
pray for money, lots of money, and even more money. One day,
it seemed that Pat's prayers had been answered.

Pat dreamed that there was gold buried under a large flagstone
just outside Desmond Castle in Askeaton. At first Pat took no
notice of the dream, but when he had the same dream a second
night, and then a third, he knew he must go out and seek the
fortune that awaited him.

He told two men, and they agreed to come with him the next
night to dig for gold. Bringing a pickaxe, a shovel and a lantern,
they arrived at Desmond Castle at the stroke of midnight.
They looked for the flagstone and, having found it, began to dig.

Suddenly there was a terrifying noise behind them. Looking
around, they saw a gigantic black bull that had its eye on them.
As the bull came charging towards them, the men dropped their
tools and ran as fast as they could towards the castle and hid there.
Peering out to see whether the bull was still after them, they saw it
had stopped at the place they were digging. It was pawing at the
ground. 'It's as if it is trying to dig too,' Pat said.

The men laughed and came out of hiding to shoo the bull away. The creature dug in its heels and would not budge. Before their eyes, the bull changed into a knight in a suit of armour, with a long sword in his hand. The warrior raised his sword and roared at the men in Irish, 'I advise you to leave now or forfeit your lives. I am the guardian of my master's treasure, and I swear I will defend it. You will not take it!'

The men did not stop to argue. They gathered their tools and went home disappointed. Next day one of the men returned to the castle, hoping to find the spot in the light of day, but he could find no flag stone, nor any sign of where they had been digging.

THE COBBLER'S DREAM

There was a man named Dick Bourke who lived around Annascaul in County Kerry. He had a dream one night that he would find great treasure at Wesley Bridge in Limerick. On the strength of that dream, he had walked all the way to Limerick. Early in the morning each day he used to walk up and down the bridge, looking for money, but he never found any.

A Limerick cobbler, who was up early one day, saw the man searching the road with his eyes and stopped to ask him, 'Have you lost something there? Will I give you a hand to look for it?'

'No,' said Dick Bourke, 'I did not lose anything, but neither did I find anything.' He told the cobbler about his dream, that he would find his fortune on Wesley Bridge.

'Away home with you, you foolish man,' said the cobbler. 'I had a dream myself that I would find a pot of gold under an apple tree in the garden of a man called Dick Bourke in Annascaul. But I'm not going chasing a fortune because I had a dream. I don't even know where Annascaul is.'

Dick Bourke said nothing, but he started walking back home to Annascaul. When he got there, he began to dig. Under the apple tree he found a flat stone with some Latin words carved on it. As Dick couldn't read Latin, he did not know what it said, so he just kept on digging. He found a pot of gold and he brought it into the house, to count his fortune.

A few weeks later, a poor scholar came to the house. When he saw the stone with its carved inscription, he said, 'That is an interesting stone, sir. The words are Latin, but I can translate it if you like.'

'Please tell me, what does it say?'

'It says, "There is another pot of gold at the other side of this tree." Does that mean anything to you, sir?'

Dick went out and started digging and it didn't take long before he found the second pot of gold. He was wealthy now and thought it would only be fair to give some gold to the Limerick cobbler who had told him where to find his own fortune.

He made his way comfortably to Limerick, in a carriage this time, and soon found the cobbler's house. Dick told the story of his good fortune, then asked the cobbler, 'How much money would you need to set up in business on your own?'

'I'd say that £100 would see me rich within a year.'

Dick gave him the £100, and said he would return in a year to see his progress. The cobbler's business became very successful, and he repaid Dick's investment at the end of the year. It seems that both men had found their fortune after all. Perhaps dreams are not such nonsense after all?

Sources

'A Golden Key': NFCS 483:118 Sean Seoghas. Foynes (B) School, County Limerick

'Hidden Treasure': NFCS 482:322; John Tobin, Shanagolden. Collector: K. Donavan, Shanagolden. Nutgrove School, Mullagh, County Limerick

'The Cobbler's Dream': NFCS 487:412–413 Michael Dalton (60), Carrikerry, Ardagh. Collector: Seamus Debruin, same address. Carrikerry (B) School, County Limerick

10

STRANGE GOINGS ON

THE NEW HOUSE

In the parish of Shanagolden there was a farmer called Pat who was doing all right for himself. He had two farms and he was building himself a new house on one of them, where an old house had fallen down.

The strange thing was that whatever he built up during the day, he'd find all torn down again when he returned the next morning. Day after day this happened, and he was sorely vexed by it.

One day there was a lad came knocking at Pat's door, looking for work. Pat said, 'I have just the job for you!' and he led the boy out to the site of the new house and showed him around. Pat told the boy, Jack, that he had been building his house, but that each night the walls were flattened down to the ground. 'Your job will be to watch over the house during the night. You will get a fair wage for the work. I will pay you £300 for every night you spend there.'

The two shook hands on that bargain and Jack got himself ready for his night watch. He brought a thick blanket with him, and built a good fire to keep himself warm and give a bit of light. He settled himself down on a log to mind the house. As all was quiet, and nothing stirred, Jack was thinking this must be the easiest job he'd ever had – and the best paid!

Just around the stroke of midnight, Jack heard footsteps approaching. As he peered through the dark, he made out the shapes of three men with hurleys in their hands. They had a fourth, an old man among them, and the three were throwing him around inside the new house.

When he saw this awful cruelty, Jack called out to the old man, 'I will do what I can to help you, sir!' As soon as he had spoken, the men all disappeared. Nothing else came to disturb the peace for the rest of the night. In the morning, Jack reported what he had seen and got his money from the farmer.

The next night Jack returned to the new house, lit his fire and settled down. Again, the three men came just after midnight. This time they carried a coffin. When they put this down to play their hurling around the house, Jack raised the lid and looked inside the coffin. Inside, he found a broom. Soon enough the men disappeared into the dark. In the morning, Jack reported what he had seen and got his money from the farmer.

On a third night, when midnight came, Jack saw the old man in the house again. He was walking up the stairs, but kept turning to Jack with a grimace on his face. 'Why are you making that strange face?' asked Jack. The old man explained that twenty years before he had been killed by three men who meant to rob him and take his gold. He said, 'In all those years, when I have returned to haunt this place, no man has spoken a single word to me. Not until you came, Jack. You are a brave lad and I will now do something good for you.'

The old man showed Jack to the doorstep. 'Under that step, you will find where I hid my treasure. If you dig there, you will find three crocks of gold: two for your master and one for yourself.'

Straightaway Jack went down to the house and told the farmer what the old man had told him. They fetched crowbars and shovels and went back to the new house. After a half an hour or so, they had the step up, and dug out beneath it – and there were the crocks of gold, just as the old man had said. Jack got his money from the farmer and the crock of gold too. He left that farm a rich and happy lad.

And what of the new house? After that night, the walls were never thrown down again and after a while the farmer moved himself in and lived there in great style.

Tom and the Haunted Castle

A man called Tom lived near Carrickerry. People called him 'Tom the soldier', but he was just a poor man who had to get by doing whatever bits of low-paid work the farmers would find for him to do.

One day he met an old travelling man and the two stopped to chat together. The traveller asked Tom what work he did. Tom explained he had bits of work with farmers, but that it was hard for him in the wet and cold weather, when his hands were stiff and sore. The traveller asked Tom if he was a man with good courage. Tom didn't know why he wanted to know, but said yes, he was brave enough in the dark of the night.

'Well,' said the traveller, 'there is a chieftain with a grand big house near Glin. They say the house is haunted, and any man who stayed the night was found dead there in the morning. Would you have the courage to stay a night in that house?'

'That I would,' said Tom, and he asked for directions, planning to speak to the chieftain the next day.

Next morning Tom found his way to the chieftain's house. He was passed from one man to another for hours before at last he got to speak to the chieftain himself.

'I hear that you have a haunted castle,' said Tom.

'That is the case,' said the chieftain. 'And I will offer three crocks of gold to any man who can sleep there for three nights.'

'Very well,' said Tom. 'I believe I am the man you are looking for.'

The chieftain gave Tom a hearty meal, then sent him on his way to the castle. Tom brought two bottles of whiskey to see him through the night. He made his way in and lit a fire in the grate, settling himself down nearby for the first night.

It was not long after midnight when Tom awoke, hearing voices outside the room. Then the door was opened, and there stood a grey man and three other odd-looking fellows in yellow coats. The grey man sat down in an armchair and the others stood around him as he asked them about a murder that had taken place in the castle years before. After a while the grey man spoke to Tom, asking, 'What are you doing here?'

'I am here to rest for the night,' said Tom, trying to keep his voice from shaking with fear. An hour later, the strange men suddenly disappeared and Tom slept for the rest of the night.

In the morning, the chieftain came knocking at the door. When Tom did not answer, the chieftain thought he must be dead, as many before him. He knocked again, louder, and this time Tom arose and opened the door.

'Well, man, what did you see and hear in the night?' asked the chieftain.

Tom told his story of the men who came in the night.

'And will you stay a second night?'

'I will,' said Tom, 'but I will need another bottle of whiskey with me.'

Tom returned to the castle that night, made up the fire, and settled himself close by. Close to midnight, it seemed a mighty storm was raging outside and the whole castle began to shake. Then came a knocking at the door. He did not answer it, but suddenly the door burst open. There were four big strong men, holding down another man. The four pushed the other man into an armchair, and sat him there.

Tom was feeling quite afraid and took a good drink of his whiskey for courage. The door opened again and another strange man came in. This one spoke, saying it was getting late, and it was now time they left the castle. The men all left and, wondering what else could possibly happen that night, Tom went over to the window to look outside. Before he could see anything, he was hit over the head and fell to the ground. When he came round, he settled himself by the fire and slept through the rest of the night.

In the morning, the chieftain came again knocking at the castle door. Tom rose and opened the door and the chieftain was surprised to see him alive. He asked what Tom had seen and heard in the night and Tom told his story of the night-time visitors.

This time the chieftain invited Tom to his house, where he gave him a great meal. The two went walking through the parkland around the palace to pass the day. Then the chieftain asked Tom if he would dare to spend a third night in the castle.

'I will,' said Tom and, fetching another bottle of whiskey, he set off for the castle. He made up the fire and settled himself down nearby. Tom slept for an hour or two, but was woken by a sudden noise. He saw all the windows shaking and thought the whole castle might fall in ruins around him. Then four men came in through the window, carrying a coffin on their shoulders, which they placed on a table in the middle of the floor. They lifted the lid of the coffin and a withered old man sat up in it. The four who had brought in the coffin left by the window again, leaving the old man behind. After a while Tom spoke, asking the old man, 'What is your business here?'

The old man just stared at Tom, until at last he lay down again in the coffin. The four men returned, fastened on the lid, and left again through the window, carrying the coffin on their shoulders.

Tom went to the window and from there he saw a crowd walking in procession behind the four coffin bearers. One man spoke to him, saying that he should join the funeral. Tom went out and he had to take his turn at carrying the coffin. It seemed to grow heavier and heavier, till Tom thought he would be flattened beneath it. 'Won't someone give me a hand?' he called out. All had gone quiet around him. Then he heard a mad wild laughter, which faded away into the dark.

Tom went back inside, settled himself down by the fire, and soon was asleep once more. He did not wake until the morning, when the chieftain again came knocking at the door. The chieftain asked Tom what he had seen and heard that night.

'Oh, it was the worst night I have spent in a long time,' said Tom, and he told his whole story.

'Will you come now to my palace and take your ease?' asked the chieftain.

'I am too tired to move,' said Tom. So the chieftain sent for his carriage to bring him there. Tom spent three days and nights in luxury in the palace, and at the end of that time the chieftain gave him the three crocks of gold he had promised.

Tom went home to Carrickerry a rich man and he lived a life of leisure from that day on. From time to time he would go to visit his friend the chieftain, and they would laugh about the three nights of terror that Tom had spent in the castle. Tom was the only man who ever had the courage to stay there.

A GHOSTLY FORTUNE

An old man once lived near Templeglantine who was known locally as Williamín. Williamín was a small, shrunken old fellow who, by this time in his life, had no home of his own, but lived with his good neighbours called Murphy. The man of the house had a brother who had long since emigrated to Canada, promising that one day he would return and bring with him a great fortune. This brother wrote long letters, and Williamín always read them, delighted to get the news.

One day the post brought a letter with news of the brother's imminent return. The whole household was excited to welcome him home, and to share in his good fortune. Williamín decided to go out and greet the returning brother in a wood he must pass through on the way home.

The night of the brother's return drew near, and all sat up eagerly awaiting his arrival. The fire was burning brightly, the kettle steaming away, the bed made up for the honoured guest, and a seat drawn up beside the fire for him.

Williamín took up his lantern and went out into the wood to wait, hiding in the bushes. Soon enough the man came by, but when he heard Williamín behind him, the man ran into an old mansion. There he hid his purse of money under a flat stone, and came back out again. Williamín was baffled: what was the man doing at all? He took up a stick and struck the man, who crumpled to the ground. What had he done?

Williamín searched under everywhere for the purse of money, but could not find it anywhere. He rolled the man's body towards the river, and pushed it into a deep pool. Then Williamín went home – without either the man or the money – and told the man of the house that the brother had not shown up at all that night.

After that dreadful night, Williamín hardly slept at all. His foul deed came back to haunt him as he lay alone in his little loft bed. His dreams were filled with the face of the man he had killed in the wood.

Many years later, one stormy night, Williamín made his way through the woods towards the old mansion. As lightning split the sky, he knelt beneath an old oak tree and cried out a prayer asking forgiveness for the murder. Williamín wept on the sodden ground, as thunder and lightning danced around him.

The man of the house and his son went out to search for Williamín. Where could he be wandering on such a wild night? They searched high and low, until at last they found him on his knees, praying under the oak tree. Williamín wept and wailed and confessed what he had done to the man's brother all those years before.

As he spoke of that terrible night, a spirit appeared and spoke to the man of the house. The spirit told him to go into the old mansion and there to lift a certain flat stone. The man did as he was instructed, and there he found the purse of gold, hidden on the night of his brother's murder. When the man said he would forgive old Williamín, the brother's spirit faded away into the night, and was never seen again. From that night on, Williamín slept soundly in his bed and wanted for nothing.

THE LIOS OF THE BLACKTHORN

The blackthorn is a tree of contrasts: its branches are dark, its blossoms white, and its fruit the bitter blue-black sloe. Covered with long thin thorns, it spreads easily and creates an impenetrable barrier to man or beast. When the leaves have fallen, it resembles a twisted skeleton, and is associated with the old hag of winter. Its wood was used for making walking sticks and cudgels.

There was an old *lios* that was used as a graveyard. People said that there had been a battle long ago and that many soldiers were buried there. When anyone was buried there, they would plant a blackthorn bush on the grave to mark the spot, but as time passed by the blackthorn bushes grew taller and spread widely throughout the *lios*. There was one blackthorn bush that always grew bigger than all the others. In the spring it would be covered in white frothy blossoms and in autumn it was heavy with bitter black sloes. The man who was buried beneath it had always carried a blackthorn stick with him wherever he went. He wanted to keep it with him in death too, and with his last breath he asked that it be buried with him. People said the place was haunted, and were reluctant to pass it by at night.

One dark night Tom was walking on the road near the *lios*. It was almost midnight, and as he got closer to it, he remembered that the place was supposed to be haunted and he began to quiver with fear. If there had been some other way he could get home, Tom would have turned and gone. He had no choice but to carry on.

When a sudden flash of light lit up the dark road, Tom gasped and his legs gave way beneath him. Everything went black and he fell to the ground in a faint. When he came to again, he found he was inside the *lios*. He did not know how he had got there. He sat up, rubbing his eyes because he wasn't sure of what he was seeing. There were thirty men playing a hurling match in the *lios*. Every now and then one called out another's name. They were names Tom recognised from his home district. When he looked closer, he noticed that these men were his old friends – but they had all died, some of them a long time ago. One of the men came towards him, holding out a hand for Tom to shake. Tom looked up. He would recognise that face anywhere: this was his old neighbour Joe, who had died only the week before. Tom had taken a drink at his wake only a few nights before! He stood up and reached for his old friend's hand.

Another sudden flash of light and Tom fell to the ground. This time when he regained his senses, he found he was lying on the road outside the *lios*. The sun was already rising and there were drops of dew on the sharp points of the blackthorn bushes. Tom was stiff and cold, but as far as he could tell, he was still in one piece. He stood up, shook himself, and started off for home. He never took that road past the *lios* after dark again.

The Haunted House

A long time ago, there was a lovely big house, a mansion set in parkland, with long tree-lined avenues leading up to its door. There were very few other houses in that area, so it was a lonely spot. Since the last inhabitants left, the mansion had been lying empty for years. No one wanted to live there, or even go near it, because they said it was haunted. People kept away out of fear of the terrors that were said to appear there in the night.

One cold windy night, with snow falling on his cold shoulders, a tramp came wandering along the road that passed the old house. He knew nothing of its story and when he saw there was a window open, he thought this would be a good place to sleep out of the wind and weather. He gathered up a bundle of hay from the field for his bed and climbed in through the open window. The tramp was so tired from walking the roads all day long that he lay down his bundle and made his bed in the first room he came to. Before long he was fast asleep.

He slept peacefully there until midnight, when a loud noise woke him. He rubbed his eyes and found the room filled with light. Looking around, he saw a long table, piled high with platters of food. Sitting on gilded chairs around it were men and women dressed in fine clothes, enjoying their feast. Close by, there was another man

shaving in front of a mirror. The tramp drew himself into a huddle
in the corner, afraid that these grand folks might see him and his bed
of hay, and throw him out into the night. He stayed awake, watching, until they finished their feast and finally left the room. He fell
asleep once more and slept peacefully until morning.

It was still snowing when the tramp awoke. He set out along
the road, leaving deep footprints in the white behind him. A few
miles down the road he called into a cottage to beg for a cup of tea.
The woman of the house brought him in and sat him by her fire.
'It was a cold night, and there's not many houses around us here.
I hope ye found yourself some shelter, and did not have to sleep
out in the snow.'

The tramp told her he had slept in the mansion and that his
sleep had been disturbed.

'My, you're a brave man!' she said. 'There's not one round here
would choose to sleep in that haunted house. Anyone who has
spent a night there since the family left has died in the night. But
here you are quite alive. Tell me again, what was it you saw?'

The tramp told her what he had seen and she passed the word
of it around the neighbours. Such gossip has a way of spreading,
and at last it reached the ears of the relatives of the last owners.

The relatives searched high and low, and sent a message saying
they would like to meet the tramp. They offered him a large sum of
money if he would only sleep another three nights in the mansion.

When the old tramp heard this, he agreed, and went back to
make up his bed for the night. The first night, he slept in the same
room, woke up at the stroke of midnight, and saw just the same
scene as before. The next night, he moved his bed to another room.
This time, when he woke, he saw a tall gentleman with a sword in
his hand. Thinking he would be slain for sure, the tramp leapt up
from his bed. The tall man came towards him, smiling and reaching out a hand. 'Tell me, what is your business here?'

'I only came in for shelter, sir,' says the tramp, 'from the snow
and the cold weather.'

'And this is your third night sleeping under this roof, is it not?'

'It is, sir,' says the tramp.

'So, now I will tell you my business here,' says the gentleman. 'I am here to guard a pot of gold that is buried beneath the floor of this room. I will show you where to find it now. Take it and bury it within the wall of a nearby fort. A small light will guide your way, but be sure that no one sees what you do. Tell no one what happens this night.'

The tramp lifted the floorboards and there was the pot of gold! Out into the dark night he followed a little light to the old fort. He dug a hole just inside the wall and there he buried the gold, then returned to his bed in the mansion. He slept undisturbed for the rest of the night.

When the relatives heard that the tramp had slept there undisturbed, they came to the house. If it was no longer haunted, then they would move in and live there themselves! They threw the old tramp out into the cold. They had no more need of him, after all.

But now the tramp knew the secret of the pot of gold. He returned to the old fort, dug up the gold, and he was never without a comfortable bed in a warm house after that night.

A TREASURE FOUND

Almost every parish has its stories about men who go digging in the night for treasure in caves, in ring forts or in the grounds of old mansion houses. In the ring fort of Reerasta (Rí Rásta) near Ardagh, there really was treasure found, which is now proudly displayed in the National Museum of Ireland in Dublin.

During the penal times, country people used to gather at mass rocks on hills and moors and the priests would say the mass out in the wilderness. The fort at Reerasta was used for this purpose. Long before those times, church treasures were often buried in out-of-the-way places for safekeeping from Vikings and other plunderers. Sometimes such treasures were never recovered by those who concealed them. Perhaps they took the secret of their hiding places to their graves.

In 1868 two lads, Paddy Flanagan and Jim Quin, were digging up potatoes within the ring fort of Reerasta, when their spades struck something hard. Filled with curiosity, they scrabbled in the dirt, clearing away the soil to reveal a flat stone covering a small bronze chalice and some silvery brooches. This was treasure all right to a couple of farm lads, but when they dug a little deeper, they found something even more extraordinary. There was a second chalice, and this one was made of silver, decorated with gold filigree, glass and crystal and with intricate interlace designs. It was a rare find, a shining example of Irish art and craftsmanship, comparable to the Book of Kells or the Tara Brooch.

The boys brought it home to Mrs Quin, who sold it to the Bishop of Limerick. He in turn sold it to the National Museum of Ireland, where it is still one of their key treasures.

The chalices dated to the eighth century and the brooches to the ninth century. They may have been buried to protect them from Viking raiders in the ninth or tenth century and never recovered until Paddy and Jim's discovery nearly 1,000 years later.

Why were the lads digging potatoes in an old fort anyway, you may be wondering. The land was owned by the Sisters of Mercy and Jim's mother rented it from the nuns. Mass used to be said in the fort during the penal times, so perhaps it was known as a place of safety that could offer some protection from the blight that had devastated the potato crop during the famine.

Those were hungry times in Ireland, yet those who found the treasure do not seem to have benefited from it much themselves. The two lads who found what is now known as the Ardagh Chalice remained poor. One was buried in a pauper's grave near Newcastle West, while the other took the ship to Australia in hope of a better life.

THE ROCK OF THE CANDLE

Near the village of Clarina there is a ruined castle, half hidden by ivy, at Carrigogunnell. Sitting on a volcanic crag it would have commanded a clear view over the countryside around. The castle ruin has a rich and varied history, but before the castle was built, a legend tells us that a sorceress named Grana lived on this hill.

Massive in size and terrifying to look upon, the hag Grana wreaked havoc on the land and people. She would light a candle and keep it burning in her tower every night. Even such a small light could be seen for miles around in the darkness. But Grana's candle was no beacon of light to aid travellers on their journeys. On the contrary, it was an accursed light, causing anyone who saw it to shrivel and die before the sun rose the next morning.

As a result, people were greatly afraid and few in the area would venture out at night. Instead they would block up their small windows and keep their doors closed, lest they should catch a glimpse of Grana's candle. They called the hill the 'rock of the candle' and warned travellers not to look in that direction if out at night.

Word of this awful desolation and terror spread. At last it reached the ears of the Fianna, that bold party of heroes who had sworn to set right oppression wherever they found it. One of their number, named Regan, volunteered to right this wrong.

'I will climb the tower and put out the witch's light.'

'This enchanted hood will help you to reach the tower unseen,' said Finn. 'There is a charm on it that will render you invisible.'

Regan put on the hood and the Fianna laughed as he disappeared from their sight, yet still moved among them, nudging one and tricking another.

'More than that,' said Finn, 'it will also protect you from the fateful light. You will be able to see your way, but not see the candle itself.'

Regan left the party and rode by night to Carrigogunnell. He removed his cloak, let the magic hood fall over his face, and climbed the steep rock, then scaled the tall tower itself. Good fortune was with him, for Grana had neither seen nor heard him.

Regan seized the candle and threw it down into the River Shannon, where it sank, extinguished with an almighty hiss. Steam rose like mist from the river.

Somehow, in that moment, the enchanted hood fell from his head. Regan saw the outraged Grana at the same moment that she glimpsed him. Her arms were grabbing for him to throw him into the river, just as he had hurled her light. Regan fled, taking one almighty leap and landing 2 miles west. The hag, in her fury, used all her strength to tear off a giant lump of rock and hurled it after him. Grana's aim was not her strong point. The rock crashed to the ground, missing Regan, who was well on his way back to Finn with his mission accomplished.

The crag fell in Corcanmore and the rock itself is known as Cloughregan or Regan's stone. They say that the print of Grana's five fingers can still be seen on it. Grana disappeared into the dark, and was never seen again, now that her magic light was dead.

THE CLEVER THIEF

There were two brothers who lived near each other, but in very different circumstances. One brother was rich and the other was poor, and the poor man worked for his wealthy brother.

The poor man's son was growing up and the father thought it was time that he learned a trade so he could make a good living. He went to the big house and spoke to the rich man, who said, 'Let him be a thief.'

'There's an idea,' said the poor man, a little uncertainly, 'I will make a thief of him.'

When he went home from his work that night he spoke to his son. 'Your uncle says you could make a living as a robber.'

'I will give that a try,' said the son, and off he went without a word to anyone about where he was going. A few weeks later he returned home.

The poor man was working up at his rich brother's house. He told his brother, 'My son is back home already, but surely he can't have learned his trade in just a few weeks?'

At the end of the day, the rich man said, 'Tell your son he must steal a horse out of the stable, with a jockey on his back, and two guards at the door.'

That sounded like an impossible task, but the poor man passed on the message to his son.

'That's simple enough,' said the son. 'I should be able to manage that.'

The next day the son bought a gallon of whiskey and dressed himself in torn and ragged clothes. He went to the rich man's house that night. There was a big old sow sleeping outside. He poked at her until she woke up and she made a terrible din at being disturbed. The two guards came running to see what all the noise was. 'I was asleep in the ditch and that big pig woke me up,' said the son. 'I won't get back to sleep now without a drink. Here, I have a bottle of whiskey, will you take a drink with me?'

The guards were happy to have a drink with him. They sat around laughing and drinking with the son, who took not a single drop himself. The guards got so drunk they fell fast asleep in a heap. While they were sleeping, the son called over the jockey, and offered him a drink too. He got so drunk that he fell off the horse, and the poor man's son walked away with the horse. Just as he had said, it was simple.

The next morning the father went to his work at the big house as usual. The rich man said, 'I see your son did that job very well last night. His next task is this. Tomorrow, he must steal a horse from under the plough while a man is busy ploughing.'

The father passed on the message to his son that evening, wondering how he could ever manage that. 'Very well,' said the boy, not worried at all, because he had already hatched a plan.

In the morning, the rich man set one of his servants to plough a field. The son went out and caught three rabbits, and brought them down to the field. He waited till the ploughman had worked one length of the field. Then he bent a rabbit's leg and let it go. The ploughman saw the rabbit, but he carried on ploughing. When he came round the second time, the son bent a leg on a second rabbit, and let it go. When he did the same again a third time, the ploughman said to himself, 'If all the rabbits here have a bad leg, it will be no bother to catch one.' He left his horse in the field and ran off after the rabbit, thinking of the pie his mother would make for him that night.

While the ploughman was away chasing rabbits, the son unhitched the horse from the plough harness and rode home on its back.

That evening his rich uncle was delighted that the boy had passed this second trial. He told his brother, 'I will set one more test for your son, and it will be the hardest yet. Tonight he must steal the sheet from my bed, while my wife and I are asleep in it.'

The man told his son what he must do. 'Don't worry, Father,' the son said, 'I will think of something,' and before long he came up with a plan.

The son waited until it was dark, then went to the graveyard. His other uncle had died and was buried just a few days before. He dug up the corpse and brought it up to the rich man's house. He climbed onto the roof with the body on his back. Down below in the bedroom, the rich man could hear the racket up on the roof. He got up out of bed and reached for his shotgun. Up on the roof, the son was lowering the dead man down the chimney when he saw his uncle had a gun. He hid himself behind the chimney, and when the shot came, he let the dead man drop.

The rich man called to his wife, who was still in bed, 'He is finished now!' and he carried the corpse out to bury him.

While he was gone, the son came into the house and up to the bedroom. The wife called out, 'That was quick. Have you buried him already?' thinking it was her husband.

'No, I just forgot I need a sheet to wrap him in.' He pulled the sheet from the bed, and went out again. He had only just gone when in came the rich man.

'Have you buried him already? You were only here a minute ago,' said the wife.

The rich man looked at the bed. 'I don't believe it! It's gone!'

'What is gone?' asked the wife.

'The sheet!'

Next morning the poor brother came to work as usual. The rich man said, 'Your son has learned his trade all right. He is a master thief, and has me soundly beaten.'

After that the rich man shared half his lands and his wealth with his poor brother. Now the master thief had no need to use his trade to make a living after all.

Away with Me!

Long ago there was a man who lived in Tournafulla and one day he went to the fair in Rathkeale to sell his cow. Since he would be in the town, his neighbour gave him a letter to post to an aunt living in Dublin. It was a long way to walk, driving the cow before him, and it would be a long walk home again. After he had sold the cow, and done whatever other business he had at the fair, he stopped at a house to ask for lodgings for the night. The old woman of the house said he was very welcome to lodge there. She showed him where he could sit by the fire until it was time for his bed. He saw a table set with six cups and plates. On the wall there were hooks and seven red caps hanging from them.

Six women in fine dresses came and sat at the table to eat their dinner. The old woman asked him if he was hungry, and she gave him a hearty meal. After he had eaten, she showed him to where he would sleep in the loft above and brought him a drink. 'That will help you sleep,' she told him, but he spilled half of it down his shirt and although he was tired and a little drunk by now, he did not sleep yet.

He thought the six women were up to something and he was curious to know what it was. He watched from his loft bed as each of them took a cap from the hooks on the wall and put it on. One after the other they called out, 'Away with me!' and disappeared through the keyhole of the door.

The man got out of his bed and put his clothes back on. He climbed down the ladder and took the last red cap from the wall and put it on. 'Away with me!' he called out, not knowing where he'd be away to. Just like the six women before him, he was suddenly flying through the keyhole after them. They flew through the night all across the country. Below he could see mountains and lakes, forests and rivers. At last they came to rest in Dublin. He followed the women into a public house, and the women sat there drinking all night long. He settled himself down on a bench and had a few drinks himself – well, what else could he do?

When morning came, the women put on their caps again and called, 'Away with me!' Again, they disappeared through the keyhole of the door.

The man called out, 'Away with me!' but nothing happened. He had forgotten all about the cap. He was banging and rattling at the door trying to get out, but the door was locked. The people of

the house got up to see what all the noise was, and they found him. Thinking he was a robber, they called for the guards, who said they would put him away in the jail. As they marched him along the street, it was cold now and he put his hands in his pockets. He found the letter there his neighbour in Tournafulla had given him to post to an aunt in Dublin. He read the address and found he was outside that very house. He asked the guards would they mind if he delivered his neighbour's letter while he was passing. They said he could.

He knocked on the door, and as he put his hand in his pocket for the letter, he discovered the red cap. He had forgotten all about the cap! He quickly handed over the letter, then pulled on the red cap, calling out, 'Away with me!' All at once he was flying through the air and all across the country.

This time he did not stop until he was back in Tournafulla in his own house.

SOURCES

'The New House': NFCS: 482:423. Patrick Scanlon, Kilcolman, Ardagh. Collector: Patrick Tobin, Shanagolden, Nutgrove School, Mullagh, County Limerick

'Tom and the Haunted Castle': NFCS 488:437– 447 Michael Ahearne, Carrickerry. Collector: John Dalton, Carrickerry, County Limerick. Scoil an Chúrnánaigh, Newcastle West

'A Ghostly Fortune': NFCS 488:405. William Moloney, Templeglantine. Collector: Daniel Moloney, same address. Scoil an Chúrnánaigh, Newcastle West

'Lios of the Blackthorn': NFCS 514:196. Bridie Stanton, Castlequarter, County Limerick. Coill Bheithne (C.), Baile Mhistéala

'The Haunted House': NFCS 525:108 Collector: Martin Moloney, Dooradoyle, County Limerick. Ballymartin School, Croom, County Limerick

'Rock of the Candle': NFCS 527:412. Tervoe (C)

'Clever Thief': NFCS 485:74–77. Denis Ahern. Collector: Ciaran Ahern, Athea, County Limerick. Rathsenan, Cratloe West

'Away with Me': NFCS 492:145. Kate Sheehan, Tournafulla. Collector: Betty MacCarthy. School: Gleann Gort NCW

11

TORYHILL

Toryhill may not be the highest hill in the county, but this isolated limestone hill dominates the landscape of Manister, close to the town of Croom. There are remnants of an old fortress on its slopes and an ancient gold lunula or collar was found there. It is of interest geologically, for the glacial deposits and marks left by moving ice can be seen on patches of exposed rock. In the past, people imagined these forces of nature as being giant men and women who moved and shaped the earth. The limestone makes it a suitable home for plants such as yellow-oat grass and shining crane's bill and many orchids, including the bee orchid, pyramidal orchid, early purple orchid, and common potted orchid. To the north-east of the hill lies Lough Nagirra, populated with swans, ducks, geese, herons.

The following story attempts to explain how Toryhill came to be where it is now.

HOW TORYHILL WAS MADE

There was once an old woman who lived with her only son in a small cottage by the shore of Lough Nagirra, near Croom. Some said she was a witch, and perhaps she was, or maybe she was just an old woman who kept her own company, I don't know. Her son was a great one for swimming. He loved to bathe in the lake and would take every chance he could to do this, no matter what the weather.

One day, the son got into trouble out in the lake. He was hurt and could not swim for the shore. With no one to hear his cries, the boy drowned in its deep waters and his body was never recovered.

The old woman howled and cried, tearing her hair, so great was her loss. She was so stricken with grief that she vowed that she would fill in the lake so that no one else might lose their life in it.

She set off at a great pace towards Knockfeerina, a hill 6 miles to the west. There she found she had the strength to tear a mighty chunk out of the side of the hill. She put it in her apron and she set off again towards the lake, carrying the piece of hill.

The rock was heavy and it took strength of will for the old woman to keep going. She was bent almost double with the weight of it, her apron stretched and straining. She was not far from the lake shore when suddenly the strings of her apron snapped. The big rock fell to the ground, and even though she tried with all her might, there was just no way she could lift it up again.

The rock stands there still to this day, close by the lake, and the people call it Toryhill.

They say that once every seven years the boy rises up out of the depths of the lake on a white horse. He rides seven times around the lake, and then rides back into the water and is seen no more. They say that when the waters of the lake swallow him up again, the surface is covered with foam.

But how it came to be called Toryhill is another question altogether. Some say it was originally named Knockdrumassail after a Fir Bolg *chieftain. The* Fir Bolg *inhabited Ireland before the coming of the* Tuatha Dé Danann. *They were defeated at the battle of Moytura in County Mayo. Their chieftain escaped and the King of Leinster gave him lands in this area.* Cnoc Droma Asail *literally means the 'hill of the ass's back'.*

Others say that the name Toryhill dates from the seventeenth century. 'Toraidhe' *means a robber or highwayman, and a large number of such tories, raparees and thieves took shelter on its slopes when dispossessed of their properties by the order of Cromwell in 1652.*

THE ORCHARD-MAN'S GUN

All around Toryhill there were orchards, some owned by the Church. There was an orchard-man who lived in a small lean-to cabin built against the wall of the house of prayer. His job was to guard the orchards, and the stores of apples which were kept within the house of prayer.

The orchard-man told the priest that he would need a gun to help him do his job of scaring off apple thieves. So the priest got the man a gun to protect himself and the orchard.

One night the man was very tired after his long day's work, and fell into a deep sleep as soon as he reached his cabin. While he

12

FAIRIES

There was a priest in Fedamore called Father Blake. He could see the Good People and if you were to stand on the toe on his boot, you would see them too. Because he knew the ways of the Good People, he would be the man you'd call if someone you knew was taken by them. He was always prepared for them and their tricks, and he knew how to cure anyone 'taken aery'.

One night he was coming home in a cart and they ambushed him and beat him with sticks. He was left lying in the ditch and was unable to speak for twenty-four hours. When he could talk again, his first words were, 'God help you, Father Blake, for the next seven years!'

For the next seven years he was paralysed, and he could not be the priest any more. The people of the parish took care of him until he died.

TAKEN AERY

There was a young woman taken by the fairies, 'taken aery', not long after her first child was born. The man of the house had to get in a nurse to mind the child. The nurse was sitting in the kitchen and the baby was sleeping in a basket, when the young mother came in. She gently lifted up the baby and sat down by the fire to feed him. When she was done, she wrapped the child in his blanket and put him back in his cot and went out the door. For several nights the same thing happened, and the nurse watched the pale young woman come, care for her son and then go.

The next night, the nurse put a plate of bacon and cabbage in the drawer of the dresser, and settled down to watch what would happen. When the woman arrived, she saw the plate of food and ate it hungrily before she fed her son and left.

The nurse told the husband and the woman's brother what she had seen. They planned to catch her and keep her the following night. The husband and brother waited in the kitchen. When the woman came, they leapt up and caught her in their arms and held her there.

'No, I cannot stay here tonight,' she begged. 'If you can wait till tomorrow night, then you will be able to free me from the Good People. I have not had any of their food or drink since they took me, so I am not yet theirs to keep.' She told them where they could find her the next night, and they arranged a time.

When the time was close, the two men went to the old fort and waited by the gap. They watched her come out, pulled her away from the Good People, and carrying her between them, they ran for home as fast as they could.

The nurse made sure she ate and drank and slept the next few days, until she was her old self again. She never spoke about what she had seen in her time with the Good People, in fact she did not speak much at all after that. But her child had his mother back at least, and she loved and cared for him well.

A Wife Taken – and Restored

Long ago there was a man and wife with two children who lived near Patrickswell. All seemed well and happy, at least until one terrible day when the wife suddenly fell sick and died. The poor man had been out working all day and came home to find his wife lying on the floor. What was he to do now, with two children to care for, and yet he must be at his work? He made the best of it and continued to go to his work, leaving the children at home to cope as best they could until his return in the evening. He noticed that when he did return home, the children were looking well fed, clean and tidy, just as if their mother was still looking after them. Thinking this a little strange, he asked a neighbour to help him discover what was going on. So instead of going to work the next morning, the man and his neighbour hid themselves behind a wall and waited to see what would happen. It was not long before they saw a woman go into the house. They peered in through the window to get a closer look. When they saw her face, it looked just like the man's own dear wife. Could it really be her? Had he not been to her funeral just a short while before?

The woman swept the floors, did a bit of washing, fed the children and washed the dishes afterwards. When it came near the time the husband would usually return from his work, the woman wrapped a shawl around her shoulders and went out the door. The husband caught her in his arms, crying, 'I thought you were dead!'

'Oh my dear,' she cried, 'I cannot stay. I was taken by the good folk to their rath. They are not cruel, so I can come each day to care for our children. But please do not hold me, I cannot stay. I must be back in the rath by nightfall.' Saying that, she was gone.

The man's neighbour suggested he visit an old wise woman known for her charms and cures. Next day he went to see the old woman and told her his story. 'Is there anything I can do to get her home for good?'

'Yes, but you will need courage. If you go to the bush by the edge of the rath on May Eve, and take with you a bottle of holy water and a pot hook, you may be able to bring her away with you.'

'Tell me, what must I do?'

'Stand before the bush. Make a circle around yourself with the holy water. The Good People will come out of the fort and your wife will be among them. You must throw one end of the pot hook and catch her with it. Draw her into the circle of protection with you. No matter what happens, whatever you see or hear, I warn you, stay inside the circle until the dawn. If you can do that, she will be free from their spell.'

The following night was May Eve so he set out for the fairy fort, taking the pot hook and the holy water. He did just as the old woman said. As soon as he saw his wife, he caught her with the pot hook and pulled her into the circle. The Good People set to wailing and moaning, dancing around them, reaching towards his wife with claw-like hands, trying to pull her back to themselves. He held her close, knowing they were safe within the circle of protection, if only they could withstand the terrors until morning!

That night seemed to last forever. When at last the sky grew light, the pair could make their way home and had no further trouble from the Good People.

THE BLACKTHORN STICK

Long ago there was a man who was a maker of blackthorn sticks. He had a great skill in his work and a good eye that could see when a particular curve or stretch of blackthorn would lend itself to the making of a beautiful stick. He dressed and treated the wood so well that his blackthorn sticks fetched a good price, and he was known as a skilled craftsman.

One day he was passing a rath or fort and noticed a particularly beautiful blackthorn bush from which he could make a truly magnificent stick. He immediately set off home to fetch his saw and raced back to cut the stick.

In those days, the people used to say that you should never interfere with an old rath or a *lios*, that some danger would befall you if you cut a tree there. This thought was in his mind as he cut the blackthorn stick, but his desire for the beautiful thing he could imagine himself making was even stronger than his fear. It was only superstition, after all, wasn't it?

With the stick cut, he brought it home and set it up the chimney for a while to season before he would start work on shaping it.

A few days later he began to feel unwell. Day after day he grew worse, until he was unable to get out of his bed at all. His wife sent for the doctor, but he was unable to say quite what was wrong. He had never seen a case like this before and at last he declared he could do nothing for the man. The wife was distraught, for she knew now that her husband was dying.

A few days later an old tramp was passing on the road outside the house. When he was outside the door, suddenly he came over in a faint with hunger and fell to the ground. The wife went to help him up, brought him into the house and made him a cup of tea and a bite to eat. He was soon feeling better, quite revived. While they sat by the fire, talking of this and that, the wife told him of her troubles. She told him how her husband had been three weeks in his bed, and that now his skin was breaking out in a strange rash, that looked like buds breaking out on a bush in the springtime.

'That sounds a very unusual rash,' said the old man. 'Would you mind if I take a look at him? In my years of wandering I have learned a thing or two from travellers on the road. I might know something that can help. You have treated me so well, let me try to repay that kindness.'

The wife brought him into the room where the man lay sick in bed. The old man looked at the strange little growths that spread all over the sick man's body. He shook his head. 'I am sorry but I have never seen anything like this before. I do not think I can help at all.'

He went back to the seat by the fire and rested there a few minutes, wondering was there anything at all he could offer the poor couple. As he watched the flames, his eye was drawn to a stick standing in the chimney. He noticed that the buds that covered the blackthorn stick were just the same as those on the sick man's body! There must be some reason for this, but what could it be?

He went back into the sick man's room and asked him about the stick in the chimney. What was it doing there? Where had it come from? The sick man told him all about the day he had cut a stick from a blackthorn bush in the rath and set it in the chimney to season.

'Well, there is your answer!' said the old man. He turned to the wife and said, 'You must take that stick and return it to the rath, and your husband will soon be his old self again. Go now, as soon as you can. If you leave it where it is, even for a moment longer, he will surely be dead within a day or two!'

Straightaway the woman of the house took the stick back to the rath. She thought she heard voices laughing and whispering around her as she laid the stick on the ground, but maybe it was only the breeze in the branches. She did not stop to find out, but quickly went home to see if there was any improvement in her husband.

The old man was waiting for her at the door. 'Is it done?' he asked.

'It is,' said she, 'and how is he?'

'Go on in and see for yourself.'

There was her husband sitting up in the bed, rubbing his eyes as if he had just woken from a deep sleep and no sign of a rash of buds on his skin. From that day on he regained his strength and was soon his old self again. But he never again cut a stick from within a rath or a *lios*. Now he knew better and he would leave those fairy places well alone.

Tom McCarthy and the Fairies

There was a man around Patrickswell named Tom McCarthy who had a pig he'd been fattening up to take to the fair in Adare. A fine creature it was and Tom was certain he'd get a good price for it. It was December and the days were cold as well as short in length, so Tom wrapped up warm and set off with his fine pig up on his cart. He sold the pig for a good profit and so treated himself to a drink with his cronies before setting off for home.

With the warmth of his drink inside him and his heavy coat outside, Tom hardly felt the cold as he made his way back home. There were no cars in those days and Tom drove his donkey and cart through the night on the long dark road to Patrickswell. It was slow progress along that lonely road, with not so much as the moon or even the light of a single star to guide him.

He must have been about halfway home when suddenly Tom heard footsteps behind him. He spun around and there was a small man in a long black coat, a three-cornered hat upon his head, a long beard, and a broad smile upon his face. 'Is that Tom McCarthy from Patrickswell, with his ass and cart?'

Tom looked the little fellow up and down in case it was someone he knew, but he could put no name to the stranger. 'It is,' he said, as he called his donkey to a stop on the dark road.

As Tom stood still, there came up another little man, and another, and another, and another, until there was a whole crowd of them gathered around Tom on the dark road. They were all dressed the same, in long black coats, with the three-cornered hats, but they were not smiling. Instead their faces were grim. Tom could see that four of them were carrying a coffin.

The leader of the small men stepped forward and said to Tom, 'We need you to carry this coffin as far as the graveyard.'

Before Tom could say a word, the four corpse bearers had lifted the coffin and deposited it in his cart.

'Now get up there beside it,' they ordered him.

Tom climbed up and sat in the cart alongside the coffin. One of the strange men led the donkey along the road towards the graveyard, while the rest of them formed a solemn procession behind the cart.

At last they reached the gates of the graveyard. Here they took down the coffin and told Tom to go home, as his work for them was done.

It was late in the night, and with darkness all around, Tom had no idea where he was at all. He thought it would be best if he just stayed on that same road, hoping that daybreak would show him where he was.

Tom walked on, leading his ass and cart, until the sun's light began to colour the sky. Then he came to a bridge and he recognised it as the bridge of Croom. He was only 7 miles from home.

When Tom reached home he had a story to tell of the night he met the fairies on the lonely road from Adare.

FEET WATER

There is an old tradition that the water you have washed your feet in should be thrown out the door at night. They said that if the 'feet water' was kept inside the house it was almost an invitation for some evil thing to enter.

A woman living in East Limerick had a lot on her mind one evening. Her husband had died recently and her daughter was not much help around the place. She was so tired this night, that when the two of them were going to their beds, she left a broken bowl sitting on the dresser and she forgot to put out the feet water.

They hadn't been in bed long when they heard a knock at the door. 'Who is calling at this hour of the night?' they wondered.

Then they heard a voice calling 'Key, key, open the door and let us in.'

The widow and her child said nothing, but wondered who or what was at their door, feeling that whatever it was, it was up to no good.

The voice called again, 'Key, key, open the door and let us in.' This time, the key called back, 'I can't let you in. I am tied to the old woman's bedpost.'

The voice called again, 'Feet water, feet water, let us in.' This time, the feet water spilled out of the basin and flowed over the kitchen floor and under the door. The door opened wide and in came three small men with sacks of wool and three small women with spinning wheels. They sat themselves down close to the fire and this is what they did: the men brought out handfuls of wool from the sacks and carded it; the women were spinning it into yarn; then they wound it up into skeins and the men put it back in the sacks. This went on for hours through the night, and the widow and her child were scared to bits.

Suddenly the girl had a thought to go and see the wise woman who lived not too far away. She got up out of bed and down the ladder to the kitchen. There she picked up a bucket saying, 'That must be thirsty work you're at there. You'll be needing a cup of tea. I'll just go and fetch some water from the well.'

The little spinners paid her no heed. They never turned their heads from their work, but they didn't try to stop her. Out the door she went and ran all the way to the wise woman's house. The old woman was up and waiting at the door for her. The girl told her story.

'Oh that sounds bad all right. It's as well you've come to me for there's not many would know how to deal with those folk. They don't belong in our world, but I know where they are from and how to send them back there. Here's what you have to do ...'

The girl listened carefully and, having thanked the wise woman, she ran back home.

She filled her bucket with water from the well and went back towards the house. Just before she turned the corner of the house she cried out at the top of her voice, 'Sliabh na mBan is on fire! Sliabh na mBan is on fire!'

When they heard that, all the little men and women came flying out the door and headed east towards the fairy mountain of Sliabh na mBan.

The girl went into the kitchen and took up the basin with the feet water. She threw the water out over the doorstep. She set the bolt and barred the door. Then she and her mother went back to bed.

They were just nodding off when they heard feet and voices outside. 'Key, key, open the door and let us in.'

'I told you already, I can't let you in. I am tied to the old woman's bedpost.'

'Feet water, feet water, let us in.'

'I cannot,' said the feet water, 'for I am spilled on the ground under your feet.'

Well, the little folk were raging outside the door. They called to the door bolt and the wooden beam that barred the door, but they were fast in place and would not open the door for them. In the end there was nothing they could do but go back to Sliabh na mBan.

That was the first and the last time the widow and her daughter had a visit from the fairies from Sliabh na mBan. Every night after that, no matter how tired, they always remembered to throw out the feet water and tidy the kitchen before they went to bed.

THE DARK ROAD HOME

When your own two feet were the only transport you had, you'd always want to know where there was a way you could take to shorten the road. There was a woman walking home from Limerick to Ballyea who took a shortcut through the grounds of a big house belonging to some grand gentleman. As she was passing the house, a woman dressed all in white gestured to her from the gate and held out three red apples toward her. They looked firm and juicy, but feeling sure this woman was one of the Good People, she turned her face away and kept on walking as if she hadn't seen her at all.

She noticed another woman a little way ahead, who seemed to be going in the same direction. Feeling a little anxious now as the sun was setting fast and it would soon be dark, she walked a little faster, to see if she could catch her up. It would be good to have company on the lonely road. No matter how fast she walked, the other woman was still out of reach.

There was a bridge ahead over a stream that crossed the path. When the first woman set foot on the bridge she vanished into the dark as if she had never been there.

When the woman reached home, she nervously spilled out her story of the fairy women on the road. A cup of strong sweet tea and a seat by the fire warmed her through, but she swore she would not go walking the road alone after dark again.

How the Forget-me-not Got Its Name

Once a very poor man met a *lurgathan* and asked him for his pot of gold. The little fellow tried all his tricks for getting away, but it was no use for him. The poor man held him fast and begged him to give him help as he was very poor.

At last the *lurgathan* gave him a pretty little blue flower and told him to take it to a certain spot in the mountain where there was a hole and put this little flower into the hole, and he would see what would happen.

The man took the flower and let the little fellow off. When he put the flower into the hole a door opened as if he had opened a lock, and taking the flower in his hand again he went in the door into a cave in the side of the mountain.

Inside was every kind of treasure, boxes of golden coins, golden ornaments, and every kind of glittering jewel. He hardly knew what to take, but at last he filled each pocket he had with what he considered the best of what was there. He then turned to go home and was at the door when the voice called out, 'Don't forget the best of all!'

Thinking he was leaving something of very special value amongst the treasures he turned and examined each heap. He took from each what he thought the best, and turned to go home again, but again the voice warned him, 'Don't forget the best of all!'

A second time he went to each chest of treasure, and picked from each what he considered the best there, though by now he could hardly find any place to put them, but a third time when he reached the door came the warning voice, 'Don't forget the best of all!'

He stood and looked around him, but could see nothing better than what he already had chosen, and almost stooping with the weight of his load he stepped past the door into the light of day again. No sooner was he outside that door than his load grew very light. He thrust his hand into his pockets, one after the other, and found that all his treasure had turned to withered leaves. He turned to the door again – but it had shut fast, and now, too late, he realised that the best of all was the little blue flower which he had dropped inside the cave when he had seen all the treasure it contained. Ever since that little blue flower has been called the forget-me-not.

SOURCES

'Taken Aery': NFCS 517:219-220. Mary Meaney, Castlequarter, Fedamore

'Taken and Restored': NFCS 527:216. John Ryan, Patrickswell

'The Blackthorn Stick': NFCS 517:62. James Ryan, Herbertstown, Knocklong

'Tom McCarthy and the Fairies': NFCS 527:114. Maura Byrnes, Patrickswell School

'The Dark Road Home': NFCS 500:462 Sean Ó Cathasaigh, Ballyea, County Limerick. School: Duckstown, Rathkeale

'How the Forget-me-not Got Its Name': NFCS 507:538-540; Philip Jones, Broadford, County Limerick. Croom (C) National School, County Limerick

13

SAINTS ...

ST MUNCHIN'S CURSE

Nowadays St Munchin's church stands on Clancy's Strand, near the Treaty Stone and Thomond Bridge in the city of Limerick.

Hundreds of years before, around 700, St Munchin built the first, admittedly more humble, church in Limerick on that same site. As the saints of that time had a well-rounded education, a wide range of skills, and were usually willing to try their hand at whatever their god needed of them, St Munchin was doing some of the work himself.

St Munchin had completed a large part of the work, when he realised that his will was perhaps greater than his skill and that he needed a few extra pairs of hands to help raise up some very heavy blocks.

The labouring saint must have made quite a spectacle, for a crowd of Limerick people had gathered to watch him at work. St Munchin climbed down and asked them would they help him with the building. Every one of them was full of excuses, suddenly needing to be busy with something else at home, or in a rush to get somewhere else before the daylight was gone. Each turned away and refused to help and soon the crowd had dispersed. The saint was puzzled, why was no one willing to lend a hand?

Just then a party of country folk from Clare were about to cross Thomond Bridge. They had been in to the town for the day and were making their way home. They saw the saint's difficulty and heard him calling for help. They saw the local crowd all turn their backs on him and walk away.

The Clare men brought over their horses and asked the saint what he was needing. 'We can help,' they said. The saint gave them instructions and they all worked together to lift and place the blocks of stone. Soon the job was done. St Munchin thanked the Clare men for their assistance and held his open hands over them as he spoke a blessing.

Then he turned to the Limerick folk, some of whom had returned to watch the men at work. 'As for you, people of Limerick, it will come to pass that in Limerick the stranger will flourish, while the native will perish.'

Some say that even today, St Munchin's curse affects the natives of Limerick. Many believe they will not find success in their own hometown, and must move abroad if they wish to find their fortune.

St Patrick

St Patrick's Shoes

One day St Patrick was walking through Bruree. It was on a Monday morning. He had been travelling on foot for many days, and his shoes were the worse for wear and big bloody blisters were coming up on his poor feet. As he was passing the shoemaker's house, he stopped in to ask if they could do something for him to fix up his old brogues and extend the life of them for him.

The shoemaker told him to be on his way. 'We are too busy here just now to be fixing up shoes for an old tramp like you. Besides we have hardly any leather in the house. We can do nothing for you today.'

St Patrick wondered how they could be so busy if they had no leather to work with. The saint went on his way, limping on his blistered feet and left the town of Bruree. But he left a curse of his own for the town of Bruree. From that day on, every Monday a starling would fall to the ground from the walls of the castle, to remind the people of Bruree of their lack of kindness.

St Patrick and the Robber

It was one of those times when the rain had been pouring from the heavens day after day. When St Patrick awoke to another wet morning, he was very disappointed. He had plans for the day, but he was unable to do anything because of the rain. He cursed the rain: if only it would stop he could get on with doing his god's work among the people!

Usually in the morning the saint would give thanks to god for all the gifts that he gave so freely: clean air to breathe, food to fill our bellies, water to drink, clothes to warm us, the song of the birds of the air to lift our spirits, sleep to refresh our souls, and so on. But in his prayers that morning, the saint did not thank his god for the rain. As the day went on, there was no manna from heaven for him and his stomach growled with hunger. At last it came to the saint that it was because of his own mean thinking and forgetfulness that no food from the heavens was manifesting that day. St Patrick sat himself down and took a moment's quiet, asking himself what his god would want him to do now to make up for his lapse in gratitude? In the stillness, his god spoke to Patrick, telling him what to do. Next morning he was to step out into the waters of the River Shannon, and to stay there until the staff he carried sprouted with green leaves. Patrick accepted this as his penance and promised that he would see it through to its completion.

Next morning the saint awoke as the sun was rising. Facing east he spoke his prayer of thanks for all of creation. Then taking his staff in his hand, he strode out into the cold water of the river. He stood there, still as a statue, all day long until the sun was just beginning to sink in the west and the sky turned pink.

There was a notorious thief living in that part of the country. Nothing was safe from him and just that day he had stolen a cow from a field near the river. Now here he was driving the stolen cow before him with a long stick, when he saw the saint up to his shoulders in the river. 'Whatever are you doing, man, standing in the cold water this chilly night?'

Patrick explained that this was his penance for not thanking god for the rain the day before. He told the thief that he would stay in the river until his staff sprouted green leaves.

'If that is what your god demands of you for so small a thing, then there is surely no hope at all for me! I have been stealing from others all my life. Hardly a day has gone by that I haven't robbed or plundered. What chance is there for me? Is there anything I can do?'

'Well,' said St Patrick, 'first you must return that cow to its owner. Then step in here beside me until your own walking stick sprouts with leaves.'

The robber quickly led the cow back to the field and when he returned, straightaway he stepped into the cold water to stand alongside the saint.

The thief had only got up to his knees in the Shannon when buds swelled on his stick and on St Patrick's staff. Within moments, the sticky buds opened and green leaves uncurled, and before their eyes even flowers began to blossom and scent the night air.

The thief was astonished, but took it as a sign he was forgiven. From that day on he wandered the roads giving help where he could and he never returned to his robbing ways.

St Patrick lifted his arms and sang out a prayer of thanks, knowing his god had forgiven his own momentary lapse, and helped him turn a sinner towards a better way of living.

How Mice, Rats and Cats Came to Be

When St Patrick was travelling throughout the country, he would call into houses here and there for a bit of refreshment. People were always happy to bring him in and share what they had with him. Hospitality was the name of the game.

Back in those days, every household made its own butter and they would always have a flat tub called a 'cooler' in the kitchen. When they made the butter, after the yellow lumps had formed, the butter had to be rinsed in very cold water, to wash out any remaining buttermilk.

St Patrick had a kind of 'manna', a soft white substance that used to fall to him from the heavens above to sustain him when he was out on bleak mountainsides all alone, far away from the homes of generous folk.

One day, St Patrick was stopping at a house and to keep his manna clean, he laid the empty cooler over it to keep off the dust.

There was a serving girl in the house who thought she would like to taste a bit of the saint's manna. So while he was busy talking, she stole a lump of it and hid it under another cooler.

When the saint rose to go, he lifted the cooler, and what did they see come out from beneath it but a fine fat sow and her litter of *bonhams*. That was how the saint rewarded those good people for their hospitality.

As soon as the saint had left the house, the serving girl ran to the other cooler to see what was under it. She lifted the corner and out ran a swarm of mice and rats! There was bedlam in the kitchen as the womenfolk shrieked and leapt up on stools, waving brooms at the creatures.

'Run after the saint!' the woman of the house called to the serving girl. 'Catch him and bring him back, for surely he can rid us of these vermin!'

When St Patrick returned, he clapped his two hands together at the door of the house. His black mittens became two black cats with sleek and shining coats, who leapt to the floor and chased the mice and rats until all were caught and killed.

Ever since that day cats have been chasing mice and rats. It is probably safe to say that they have not caught them all yet!

A Generous Cow

Deep in the winter time, when Patrick was passing through a place called Ballinamina, near Kilfinnane, a poor old woman welcomed him and his lad into her home. The house was cold with no fire burning in the grate and she had little to offer them to eat, but it was shelter on a cold night and she had opened her door to them and an offer of hospitality should never be spurned.

Patrick sent the lad out to gather a bundle of rushes, and when he laid these in the grate, they burned like dry logs in the summer, and filled the room with warmth. He made lamps of the rushes too and these burned like candles, brightening the room.

Patrick then told the woman of the house to go out and milk a white cow that was standing in the yard. 'What cow?' she wondered, but she did as he said, and the cow gave her a full pail of warm, steamy, creamy milk. The old woman thought the saint must have brought the cow with him.

The cow was ready to be milked again an hour later and gave another pail full of milk. And an hour after that, she was ready again. There was so much milk, that the old woman soon began making butter and cheese and sharing her good fortune with all her neighbours. And that at a time of year when other cows were dry.

There was another old woman, who thought to trick the cow. She brought a sieve and intended to milk the cow until it was dry, but that cow that St Patrick brought was never milked dry. In the end she had to give up, as she was nearly drowning in all the milk. The generous cow continued to give a great supply of fresh creamy milk every day until the day it died.

The Galtee Serpent

The next day St Patrick set out for the Galtee Mountains, travelling by Glenbrohane and Ballylanders. There was a serpent lived at the top of the mountain, who would devour anyone who came too near him. Few dared to pass that way because of the fearsome creature.

St Patrick bound the serpent in chains and tricked him into a nearby lake, Lough Dineen, on the Limerick-Tipperary border. The saint told him it was only a temporary arrangement and that he would be freed again 'tomorrow'. Every now and then that serpent would come to the surface of the lake and in an angry voice, he would ask whoever passed by, 'Is it tomorrow yet?'

But of course, as it never *is* tomorrow, the serpent is still imprisoned there.

The Birds of Ardagh

St Patrick founded a church on the top of Knockpatrick Hill, near Shanagolden. He stayed in the area for a while after that, before he moved on to Ardpatrick. On that journey he passed through the place where the village of Ardagh is now. The saint and his men found scant welcome there, in fact many of the locals threw stones at them, beat them with sticks and tried to drive them away. St Patrick was so angry that he called out a curse upon them. He said there would be a corpse among them every Monday morning. The good people of the area were horrified when they heard Patrick's words, and they begged him to modify his curse.

'Not everyone here is cruel. There are good people among us, and we do not deserve your wrath. We heard your curse that each Monday there will be a death here. Can you not change the terms of it and let it fall on some other creature rather than the people?'

Patrick listened, and he saw the sense of their pleading, so he agreed. 'Let it be so. I will spare the people of Ardagh.'

They say that ever since then, every Monday morning, a dead bird has been found in Ardagh.

Why Dogs' Hair Lies Flat

St Patrick had been up on the hill of Knockpatrick. When he was making his way back down, a big black dog was coming up the hill towards him, slathering at the chops. The hairs on its back stood straight up to attention as the creature growled at St Patrick. Patrick raised his hand, and the dog quietened and sat before him. As he stroked the dog's back the dog's hairs flattened and they have stayed that way ever since. That is why every dog's hair lies flat to this day.

A Blessing for County Clare

When St Patrick was staying at Knockpatrick, he climbed the hill and looked out across the Shannon to County Clare. He had hoped to travel over the water and visit the county, but now he knew there was no time for this. He must travel to the north of Ireland with great speed.

With sadness that he could not walk on its green hills, he knelt on the ground at the top of Knockpatrick Hill, stretched his hands wide and sent his blessing over the Shannon. 'My blessing over you,' he called.

They say there was once a flat stone on the hill that bore the imprint of the saint's knees as he knelt to bless Clare.

The Witch's Fire

There is another story as to how that same stone got the imprint of the saint's knees.

One cold night the saint was out on Ballinacragga, on the side of Knockpatrick Hill. Although he could see the outline of houses ahead of him, he could see no light in any window. He knocked on the door of the closest cottage. No one came to the door, but at last the voice of an old woman called out to him. 'Who is there? Whatever do you want at this hour on a cold night like this?'

'My name is Patrick,' he answered her. 'I am looking for shelter on a cold night.'

The woman was reluctant, but at last she agreed to open the door to him and bring him inside. She warned him not to look up at

Knockpatrick Hill. She knew there was a witch's fire there that night, and anyone who saw it would start to sneeze and keep sneezing until they died. As she opened the door to let him in, she saw the fire on the hill, and immediately she gave a violent sneeze, 'Ah-tishoo!'

At once Patrick called out, 'God bless us!' and the fire on the hill disappeared.

The woman sneezed again, 'Ah-tishoo!', and the fire on the hill came back to life.

'God almighty bless us!' called Patrick and the fire was dowsed once again.

When the woman sneezed again, 'Ah-tishoo!', the fire on the hill blazed up brighter than ever before, the flames leaping high into the night sky.

St Patrick called out, 'God almighty bless and save us!' and this time the fire was extinguished for good. The old woman was safe now and sneezed no more.

As the saint went out into the dark, and climbed the hill, the witch threw a stone at him. Patrick knelt on that stone and the imprint of his knees remained on it.

A Curse on Stonecutters

St Patrick was just leaving Knockpatrick and was passing by the blacksmith's forge at Barrack's Cross. The forge was busy, with a crowd of men gathered outside. A group of stonecutters from Foynes had come there to get their chisels pointed. While the smith worked on their tools, the stonecutters amused themselves tormenting a poor donkey who was tied to a stone outside the forge. The poor creature was skin and bone and looked weary, thirsty, and as if it had carried loads too heavy for it to bear. The stonecutters cruelly jabbed at the donkey with their red-hot chisels. The animal simply stood there, unable to escape.

St Patrick was enraged, unable to condone such treatment of one of God's creatures. He spoke out angrily to the stonecutters for their cruelty. The stonecutters laughed at Patrick and shook their chisels at him, as if they would attack him next. Unafraid,

Patrick fetched a basin of water, and let the donkey drink its fill. Then he spoke out a curse upon the stonecutters of Foynes. 'May all stonecutters who live in Foynes, generation after generation, be cursed with a burning thirst!'

People said that even until recent times, stonecutters in that area have had a problem with drink.

St Ita

The town of Killeedy is named after St Ita (*Cill Íde* or Church of St Ita). The foster mother of the saints, St Ita was an educator, with whom many of Ireland's saints spent their formative years. She is reputed to have brought her brother-in-law back to life, after he was killed in battle, and to have restored the sight of a blind man. Her day is 15 January.

St Ita was born in County Waterford and her original name was Deirdre. Her father wanted her to marry a local chieftain, but she was determined to live a different kind of life as a holy woman. She took control in the only way she knew: she stopped eating. For three days and nights, she let not one morsel pass her lips. The next night, her father dreamed that Ita's god was talking to him. In fact he did not stop giving out to him all night long. When her father awoke in the morning, he was convinced, converted, and gave his daughter his consent. She thanked him, and went on her way to become a nun, with his blessing. She was 16 years old when she set out on her journey, along with her sister Fiona.

Lights in the Sky

As she travelled from Waterford, three lights in the sky led Ita to Killeedy, in County Limerick, where she built her community and school. The first was over the Galtee mountains; the second on the Mullaghareirk mountains and the third at Cluain Chreadhail, which was the name for Killeedy before Ita's time. When she asked for land for her community, a local chieftain offered her a large tract of land, but Ita insisted she was content with just an acre or two for a garden.

Ita built her church at Killeedy, and there she tended her garden. She kept milking sheep and goats and a few Kerry cows. The community cared for the sick and dying, the poor and the old people. Besides this Ita was also a teacher, with a great love of children. She taught a whole generation of Irish saints, including St Brendan, who spent five years with her there from the age of 1. Ita was renowned for her kindness and care, and was called the 'foster mother of the saints', and the 'Brigit of Munster'.

St Ita is said to have spoken these words: 'The fosterage of my house is not of any common child; Jesus with his heavenly company, shelters each night against my heart.'

In my own experience of visiting primary schools as a storyteller, I have met many teachers who obviously see things as St Ita did. Their warmth illuminates their teaching and makes learning a joy for many children.

In the summertime, the dairy cows were brought up to the summer pastures at Boolaveeda, near Mountcollins. Ita would travel there and back each day with a donkey. The cows and so on would be milked at the booley in Mountcollins, and she'd bring the milk back down to Killeedy in panniers. One day as Ita was heading home from Mountcollins, she heard there was a man sick in Tournafulla, so she stopped there to visit him. She left her donkey outside in a field. While she was away, two men started tormenting the donkey, prodding him with sticks. Thinking it great sport, boys threw stones at him, and their dogs came snapping at him. The poor donkey went running off towards the river, and who can blame him. All the milk got spilled from the panniers. When he leapt onto a big rock in the River Allaghaun, the donkey's feet sank into the surface of the stone, and to this day his hoof prints can be seen there, along with the saint's footprints.

When St Ita came out of the house, she could see no sign of her donkey. She looked all around and eventually found the poor tormented creature down at the river, with the milk all gone. Seeing the marks on her donkey, showing how the people of Tournafulla had mistreated him, Ita was furious and disappointed. She spoke a curse on the people of Tournafulla, that the town would never be without three things on a Monday morning for the rest of its days: a smoking chimney, a widow and a blackguard.

On another occasion, when her donkey was lame, Ita pulled a thorn from its hoof. She pointed the thorn downwards and planted it at her convent in Killeedy, where it grew into a thorn bush.

People say that if anyone who is sick stands in Ita's footprints in the rock by the river, they will get well again.

Battle Lights

There was a chieftain living near Newcastle West who kept a vigilant eye out for invading armies. He had lookout posts at Templeglantine, 5 miles away. One day one of his scouts brought news that a 5,000-strong Kerry army was camped near Abbeyfeale, and planned to attack him the next day. The chieftain went to St Ita to ask for help. When St Ita said she would ask God to help him, the chieftain went home to get his troops ready. The battle began at sunrise, and all day long it ranged around Cullina and Shanagarry. With Ita's god on his side, the local chieftan gained the upper hand and by sunset the Kerry host fled for home. Many were slain as they ran away.

Even until quite recently, lights have been seen in the area where the battle took place, dancing in the air like bicycle lamps, or running along on the surface of the grass. Perhaps it is simply a trick of the night air, like 'jack-o'-lantern', but it could be that they are the ghosts of the Kerrymen still haunting the battlefield.

St Brigit's Visit

St Brigit was on her way to see St Ita. She had travelled a long way already, and now the light was fading, she needed somewhere to rest for the night. A chieftain near Shanagarry gave her shelter in his fort. The next morning, Brigit told him stories about her god and the chieftain converted. St Brigit lifted a few rocks from the ground, and a spring well immediately burst forth that now bears her name.

St Senan

St Senan was born near Kilrush in County Clare in the year 488. Long before Senan was born, St Patrick was standing on Knockpatrick Hill blessing the people of County Clare across the Shannon. He spoke a prophecy that a child would be born who would be a great saint and bring a blessing to the people of Clare.

When Senan was a child, his father told him to stay behind one Sunday and guard the crop from crows while the rest of the family went to mass. Senan very reluctantly stayed at home. As soon as his father had gone, Senan gave three sharp blasts of a whistle and all the crows of the district came and gathered at his feet and on the branches of trees around him. Senan herded them all together, persuaded them into a shed, and locked the door. With the crops now safe from crows, he went to mass. After mass, when his father saw him there, he was very angry. 'I told you to stay home and protect our crop from crows. Why did you disobey me? What state will our crops be in now?'

'I did protect the crop, father. Don't be angry with me. Come and I'll show you,' said Senan. He led his father to the shed, and the man was amazed by what he saw there. He never forbade Senan to go to mass on Sunday again.

Senan's father wanted him to be a soldier. He sent him off to fight in a battle, but Senan objected, not wishing to harm or kill another human being. He concealed himself in a haystack. When the enemy soldiers noticed a light shining round the haystack, they found Senan. They did not fight him, because they thought he must be an angel.

Senan travelled to Rome and became a bishop. When he came back to Ireland he came up to the Shannon and landed on Scattery Island. There was a sea serpent, a ferocious beast, that terrorised the island and all around the coast, even as far as Glin. St Senan banished the monster into a lake in County Clare. On the island there lived a pagan chieftain called MacTail who wanted to keep the island for himself. MacTail challenged the saint, tried to intimidate him and threatened to kill him. Senan stood before him unafraid.

'I have the power of God behind me. You do not frighten me with your threats. It is you should be afraid, MacTail.'

MacTail replied, 'Hah! I am as much afraid of you as I am of a shorn sheep!'

When the day came that the chieftain was going to fight St Senan, a shorn sheep frightened his horse and he fell, striking his head on a rock. He was killed on the spot.

St Senan lived peacefully in his monastery on the island after that and built seven churches there. He was building a road there too, but that was never finished. The men were working away, and a woman passed by in a rush to get somewhere else. It was the custom in those days to say, 'God bless the work,' but the woman was not paying attention and did not speak the blessing. The road was never finished and St Senan banned all women from the island after that.

St Senan visited the hill of Knockpatrick and blessed the people of Shanagolden. Since then no one from Shanagolden has been harmed by thunder and lightning.

The Three Hail Mary Stones

There are three stones in the grass at the side of the road between Manister village and Lacka Cross. They say these stones once proved a theological point between a priest and a general.

There was a priest in Manister who was friendly with one of the generals in Cromwell's army. They would have philosophical discussions of an evening and the two got on well enough together despite their differences.

One day the general came into the church whilst the priest was saying the mass, and whatever it was he had to say, he was in a rush to say it. The priest held up his hand to let him know he could not speak to him right at that moment, but must first finish the mass he had begun. The general waited angrily outside the church until mass was over, then strode in to confront his friend. 'Why would you not speak to me?' He was furious to be ignored.

'I could not interrupt the mass for those good people. You surely know that I will not speak to you during the mass. Do not ask that of me, I cannot do it, but I did say three Hail Marys for the good of your soul during the mass.'

'Pah! What good are those to me? That is just an empty superstition!'

'Ah now, it must be said, those prayers will be doing you a great amount of good.'

'If that is so, then prove it to me. If you can do that, then I will spare your life. If not, then I will see you hanged!'

'Well now, in the grand scheme of things,' said the priest, 'those three Hail Marys would have the same weight and gravitas as your-self and your horse.'

'But will they indeed?' said the general. 'Go on, write your three Hail Marys here on this paper.'

The priest wrote out the prayers while the general set up three big stones for a scales at the side of the road. To his great surprise, the three Hail Marys on the paper weighed just the same as himself on his horse! So the priest was saved to speak a mass another day.

Those three stones are still there to this day, and the local people keep them clean and free from moss. They call them the 'Three Hail Mary Stones'.

Sources

PATRICK:

'Shoes': NFCS 528:316. Patrick Kelly, Kilmallock Hill, Collector: Kathleen O'Connor. Kilmallock (C) School

'Robber': NFCS 528:322-326. Patrick Kelly. Collector: Mary Savidge. Kilmallock Convent School

'Mice, Rats and Cats': NFCS 528:343. Mary Savidge. Kilmallock Convent School

'Birds of Ardagh': (p. 45, Mrs Mary Griffin, Baranigue, Carickerry, Ardagh) Volume 0482, p. 52. Glenbaun, County Limerick Cluain Leith Áird

'Dog's Hair': NFCS 483:79. J. Jackson, Foynes; Collector: Máire Ní Chonríogh. Foynes (C) School, County Limerick

'Blessing County Clare': NFCS 483:168-9, John Mulvihill, Shanagolden. Collector: Michael Mulvihill Shanagolden

'The Witch's Fire': NFCS 483:112. J. King, Foynes. Collector: Maire Ni Conroy, Foynes Girls NS

'Curse on the Stonecutters': NFCS 483:170, Tom Seran, Foynes. Collector: Eoin Carran

ITA:
NFCS 488:308; 489:160. Mrs D. Cagney. Collector: Nellie Cagney
NFCS 488:301. Michal Sullivan, St Ita's Terrace. Collector: John Sullivan

SENAN:
NFCS 483:158. Michael Curren. Collector: Eoin Curran. Shanagolden
NFCS 482:335. Teresa Walsh, Shanagolden. Nutgrove School, Mullagh, County Limerick
NFCS 483:160. Katie Madigan. Collector: Eoin Curran. Shanagolden

14

... AND SINNERS

A SPELL OF SEED SOWING

There was once an old widow woman living
near Adare in a small cottage with an acre of
land. Her name was Peig na nGort and some
of her neighbours said she was a witch.

One year Peig asked a neighbour to sow
the acre with wheat for her. The man had a
reputation as a good seedsman and he was
also an obliging sort of fellow. He agreed
that he would and, being a good neighbour to a poor old woman, he said he
would ask no payment for the work.

The man turned up on the
appointed day, and put on the
apron Peig gave him for the job.
He was ready to start shaking out
the seed, when Peig came out and laid a
small sack of wheat on the headland.

The neighbour looked at the sack of
seed, then at the acre of land. 'You surely
don't expect me to be able to cover this
stretch of land with that little sack of seed?'

'Oh,' said Peig, 'you best just work away with that for now. Give me a shout when you reach the end of it and I'll get some more.'

He scooped up the seed and filled his apron with enough to cover from here to the other headland, then set off, spreading it as he walked. By the time he reached the far headland, his apron was every bit as full as when he'd started. He turned and walked back across, spreading the wheat as he went, but when he had walked two lengths, he still found his apron full of seed. He just could not understand it. He turned and walked another two lengths, and still there was plenty of seed in his apron. The day went on the same way. He walked the length of the plot, spreading seed all the way, then turned and walked back, spreading seed again. He was nearly finished sowing the whole acre, and still his apron was full of seed.

At last he was back at the place he had started, and there was the sack of seed, just half full, as he had left it.

He did not know what magic Peig na nGort had put on the seed to make it spread so far, but he was not happy at being used in this way. He swore he would never spread seed for Peig na nGort again.

THE TINKER AND THE DEVIL

There was once a tinker living around Kilcolman who was known in the area for doing a good job of mending pots and pans. Despite his reputation for good work, he was still poor and always looking for bits of work. One day he had to go to Duncaha to mend some broken pipes. On his way there he had to walk through a large dark wood. He got straight to work, and there was nothing but praise for the job he did. When he was finished, they paid him 3 shillings.

As he was going home, he came to a crossroads. A poor man asked him if he could spare him any money. The tinker, feeling well off for a change, gave him a shilling and went on his way. 'Bless you, sir,' the beggar called. As the tinker reached the edge of the dark wood, he met another poor man, this one even more ragged and thin than the last. Could he spare any money? The tinker gave another shilling, and walked on into the wood. 'Bless you, sir,' the beggar called behind him.

On the path through the dark wood, he met a third poor man who asked for his help. The tinker did not know what to do this time. He had only 1 shilling left. He was poor enough himself, and without that shilling, how would he eat tonight? He offered the beggar sixpence. The beggar refused it. 'If that is all you can give me, you best keep it. But if you have a shilling, I would take that, and thank you.'

The tinker gave his last shilling to the poor man and walked on. What could he do now he had given away all he had? 'May the devil take me if I ever pass through this wood again!'

Suddenly, the wood filled with light. He looked around, and saw a bright angel with light around his head standing before him. 'It was myself you met three times on your path in the guise of a beggar. And as you gave me what you had so willingly, I will now give you three wishes.'

The tinker was delighted. Without stopping to think, he straightaway made his wishes. 'I wish that the village boys would never again touch my tool bag. I wish that anyone who tries to pick an apple from the tree outside my home becomes stuck to it. And I wish that my flour bin is full of flour when I get home.'

The angel said, 'As you wish, so shall it be,' and they parted.

When he reached home, the tinker looked in his flour bin, and saw that it was full. He was delighted to find his wish fulfilled, and he told his wife about his encounter with the angel.

A few weeks later he was called back to the same house in Duncaha. He set off in a great mood, thinking he would have the same adventure as before. He did the job, got paid, but on his journey home again, things did not work out quite so well for him.

Passing through the wood, he met the devil, who said, 'You must come with me. The last time you were here, you said, "May the devil take me if I ever pass through this wood again!" Don't you remember?'

The tinker now regretted his hasty curse, but what could he do? He went with the devil. When they were near the tinker's house, he turned to the devil and asked, 'Can you change yourself into another shape?'

'I can, of course,' said the devil. 'What would you like me to change into?'

'How about an iron bar?' said the tinker, beginning to hatch a plan.

The devil asked, 'Why do you want me to change my shape?'

'It's a bit embarrassing,' said the tinker. 'This is the town where I live and everyone knows me. If people see us together, they will laugh at me.'

The devil changed himself into an iron bar, and the tinker put it in his tool bag. He ran to the blacksmith's forge, got the iron bar ground up, and was free again.

A few weeks later, the tinker was passing through the wood, and met the devil again. 'You fooled me last time, but now you're coming with me,' and the tinker had no choice but to go with him. When they got near his house, the tinker said, 'Would you look at those red juicy apples on the tree by that house. Would you ever pick one for me?'

The devil went into the garden, reached up for an apple, and he stuck to the apple tree. 'Let me go! Let me go!' he demanded.

'I will not let you go until you set me free,' said the tinker, and the devil reluctantly agreed.

A few weeks later, the tinker was called to Duncaha again. As he was passing through the wood, he met the devil again. 'You fooled me before, but this time you have to come with me.'

The tinker asked if he could have time to say a few words of prayer. When the devil agreed, the tinker used that moment to make his escape. He never met the devil on his path through the woods again.

AT LORD DUNRAVEN'S TABLE

One day Lord Dunraven had invited the Catholic Bishop of Limerick to dinner at Adare Manor. There was a great party invited and, it being a Friday, of course the bishop expected the meal to be fish.

But at Lord Dunraven's table, every dish was meat. There was every type of meat you could imagine, mutton, beef, lamb, even venison, all laid out on silver salvers.

Whilst they were waiting for the feast to begin, Lord Dunraven asked his guests, 'Is there anyone at this table can perform a feat that will astound us all?'

When no one replied, he spoke again, 'Let me give you an example of what I have in mind.'

He took up a small book from his pocket and began to read from it, perhaps in Latin, or some other ancient language. While he spoke, the table began to rise into the air, covered as it was with the tablecloth and all the silver salvers and crystal. Soon it was up level with the guests' faces and moving towards the big bare window. Out the window it flew and on beyond, till it was only a speck visible on the far horizon. Lord Dunraven took out his book again, and began to read some more. As he closed up the book, the table returned, in through the bare window and down to the floor again.

Everybody cheered.

'Now my dear guests, is there one among us who can do something quite as extraordinary?'

The Bishop of Limerick stood up, opened his book and began to read. He closed his book, and spoke a short blessing over the food. 'Now, ladies and gentleman, let the feast begin!'

When they took the covers off the dishes, all of them were overflowing with fish. All the meat had vanished and only fish was served that Friday at Lord Dunraven's table after all!

A Dance with the Devil

There was a young woman called Margaret who loved to go dancing. It was the one thing that always brought a smile to her face and warmed her heart. She could put up with almost any hardship or discomfort in life, so long as she had a chance to dance every now and then. Margaret heard that there was a big dance coming up, and all her friends were going. She wanted to go too, but she didn't have a dress to wear. It was going to be a formal ball, with fancy gowns and suits. She went into the town one day, and didn't she see the most beautiful dress in the draper's shop window. It was just gorgeous, with bits of lace and ribbons on it, but when she went in and asked how much it cost, her face fell. It was just too dear. Even if she saved up for months, Margaret would never be able to pay for it.

She left the shop, but still could not take her eyes off the dress in the window. She was still standing there, dreaming about the ball and how it would be if she was there dancing in that lovely gown. Next thing, there was a gentleman standing beside her, a respect-able-looking fellow in a smart suit and hat. He said to her, 'It is a lovely dress. I see you are admiring it and I believe it would look very good on you, miss, if I may be so bold.'

'Oh it is lovely,' she said, 'but it is beyond my means to buy it.'

'Let me buy it for you,' said the gentleman.

'Oh no,' she said, 'that's a nice thought, sir, but I could not allow that. I don't even know you.' Margaret walked away and went home, without the dress.

The next day when Margaret was finished her work, a parcel arrived at the house with her name on the label. She opened it up, and what was inside but the beautiful ball gown. She tried it on, and it fitted her perfectly. It was even more lovely close up than it looked through the shop window. Now she could see the little details of embroidery and beading, how the colour of the blue ribbons matched her eyes. She could hear the swish as she walked, and see how the silk dappled like water in sunlight. It was as if it had been made just for her, and wearing it, she felt that she herself was beautiful too.

What should she do? Margaret knew it had to be that gentle-man who had sent it, but she did not know his name, and there was no return address, no card with it. She could hardly send it back. Should she keep it and go to the ball? It did not take too long to convince herself. Yes, of course she should! Off she went to the dance.

The hall was full, all the smart young people from miles around were there and all dressed up to the nines. It was a very grand affair, but didn't she just fit the bill in her new ball gown. Wearing the new dress seemed to make her stand taller, walk more gracefully. Many young men's heads turned to watch as she walked in through the crowd. Her girlfriends gathered around to admire her lovely outfit, asking, 'Where did you get that dress?' 'How could you ever afford it?' But she told them nothing.

When the band began to play, a very dapper fellow eased his way through the crowd. He was wearing a smart black suit with

a bow tie, his dark hair groomed with oil, his features handsome and a smile of admiration on his lips. Very politely, he bowed before Margaret, took her hand and asked if she would dance with him. Rolling her eyes at her girlfriends, and smiling from ear to ear, Margaret followed him onto the floor. They stayed together, dance after dance. Whatever music the band was playing, he seemed to know the steps and guided her around the dance floor. They made a stunning couple, moving with ease and grace around the hall.

Margaret, who had always loved to dance, was in her element. She had never enjoyed herself so much before, nor had she had so attentive a partner. This was surely a night to remember all her life! She thought, 'If I were to die tonight, I could not complain, for I would die happy.'

When the band stopped playing for a moment, Margaret bent down to adjust her shoe. What she saw down there made her gasp with fright. All the time they were dancing, she had not taken her eyes from her partner's face. Now, as she fixed her shoe, she could see that where his boots should have been, there were cloven hooves instead!

Margaret fell to the floor in a faint. Her friends gathered around and carried her out of the hall for air, loosening her gown so she could breathe more easily.

What became of the dapper gentleman, no one could say. He seemed to simply vanish into the night.

Margaret certainly had a night to remember and she lived to tell her tale of the night that she danced with the devil.

SOURCES

'A Spell of Seed Sowing': NFCS 526:156. Patrick Lillis, Patrickswell.
    Collector: Patrick Boland. Lurga School, Tober Padraig
'The Tinker and the Devil': NFCS 483:258 Nora O'Sullivan. Collector:
    Aidan O'Sullivan. Shanagolden (B) School
'Dance with the Devil': West Limerick Collection, CD 25, Paddy Cronin, 2003

15

DAFT NONSENSE

AN EARLY START

Two women from around Murroe decided to go to Limerick town together the next day. It would take them long enough to walk there, so they knew they would have to be up early. But back then they had no clock to tell the time of day. They said they would go as soon as the cocks crowed.

The next morning, when the cock crowed, up they got and into their decent clothes, and set off on the road to Limerick. They walked a good few miles and, needing a rest, they sat down on stones by the side of the road. The pair took out their snuff boxes and, as was the custom at that time, they said a short prayer for the poor lost souls recently deceased as they took their pinch of snuff. 'It will surely be morning any minute now,' said one to the other.

'I suppose you are right, it will be light soon, but it is still very dark yet,' said the other.

As they sat there, they heard footsteps coming up behind them. As they got closer, they saw it was a young priest, though he did look rather pale.

'Whatever brings you ladies out on the road at this hour of the night?'

'We are on our way to Limerick, and thought we would get a good start before daylight,' they told him.

'Your prayers are after sending me straight to heaven,' said the young priest, 'for didn't I die just a few minutes ago?'

The two women turned pale, realising they had met a ghost on the road. They shivered, but the young priest said, 'I can't stop to chat, but if you walk back a little way, you will find a cottage by the roadside. Go on in there. You will find a man sitting by the fire. Now, don't dare say a word until he gets up and leaves. Then you can shelter there until daybreak.'

The two went back along the road, came to the cottage, and in they went. The man was sitting by the fire, but soon he arose and went out of the door. The women sat there warm by the fire, chatting until the sun arose. But what a fright they had, meeting a ghost in the middle of the night. After that night, they never again set out for Limerick until they had enough light to see the path ahead of them.

NATURE VERSUS NURTURE

There were three brothers walking the road together. Poor scholars they were, out in the world seeking work wherever they could find it. When they reached a crossroads, they sat down on the grass and shared their food. This would be the last meal they would have together for some time. They decided they would each take a different road and made a date to meet again at the crossroads in twelve months' time.

When a year had passed, there were only two brothers who met at the crossroads. 'We will wait a day or two, in case he has been delayed,' they agreed. When he still did not come, the two agreed to meet again in another twelve months. One took the road the missing brother had taken.

Another twelve months passed and this time only one brother arrived at the crossroads. He stayed two days there, but neither of his brothers came. He took the road his missing brothers had taken.

It was a fine road and it led him to a stately mansion. When he met a gentleman he asked had he seen his two brothers who had come this way.

'Oh, I saw them,' said the gentleman. 'They came here, but they never left here.'

'What do you mean?' asked the brother, 'Did my brothers die here?'

'They did indeed,' the gentleman admitted. 'I set them a challenge to prove to me that nature can't be trained. If they could prove it, I would reward them with a purse full of gold. If not, they would forfeit their lives. Both your brothers failed, and so, yes, I killed them. Now you have come, you will meet the same fate, if you cannot prove to me that nature can't be trained.'

The poor scholar was determined he would not lose his life here. 'I will prove it to you,' he said, wondering how he would manage to do it.

He got a bit of supper and went to his bed. In the morning, after his breakfast, he helped with threshing the corn, and walked about, thinking how he could prove it. He looked around, and suddenly he had an idea. He caught three mice and put them in his pocket along with a bit of corn to keep them happy.

After a while, the gentleman sent for the poor scholar. When he entered the room, the man was sitting at a table, reading, with a large cat sitting on his lap. 'Let me introduce you to my cat, Tom, a most intelligent creature. I have trained him to do many tasks for me. Come, Tom, hold up the candle so that I can read.'

The cat lifted the candle in his front paws.

'Oh, that is very clever,' said the poor scholar, letting a mouse out of his pocket as he spoke.

As soon as Tom saw the creature, he dropped the candle and chased after the mouse.

The gentleman was not at all pleased. 'Bad Tom,' he chastised the cat. 'Take up the candle.'

The cat did as he was told, but the poor scholar let out another mouse. Again the cat dropped the candle and chased the mouse.

The gentleman was furious. He caught the cat and beat him within an inch of his life.

The poor scholar let out his third mouse, and the cat chased it, pounced on it and ate it.

'That is a very clever cat you have, sir, but it looks to me as if nature is stronger in him than all the tricks you taught him. Would you still maintain that nature can be trained?'

'I give in,' said the gentleman. 'You have proven your case and I must reward you.' He gave the poor scholar a bag full of gold coins.

The Priest's Umbrella

In the old days there were not many umbrellas around in the countryside. The first person to have an umbrella in this part of the country would have been the parish priest, to keep himself dry when he was out visiting the people.

One day he was invited out to say a mass in a very rural part of the parish. He was taken out there in a cart and, as it was raining, he brought his large black umbrella with him.

Before walking in the door, he shook the umbrella to get most of the water off it. But because it was still very wet, he left it open in the kitchen to dry.

After saying the mass, the priest stayed for tea and a bite to eat. By now the sun had come out, and the day had turned dry. The priest said his goodbyes and forgot all about his umbrella, and set off walking back to the parochial house, enjoying the fresh

air and the fine day. It was only when he reached the door that he remembered he had left the umbrella in the kitchen. He sent a messenger back to fetch it.

Back at the house the large black umbrella was a real curiosity as no one had ever seen such a thing before. When the messenger arrived asking for it, they could not get the umbrella out through the kitchen door. They tried turning it this way and that, but it just did not fit in the doorway. They wondered how had the priest got it in there in the first place? Back then the windows were very small, so there was no point in trying to take it out that way.

'We could take off the door, that might make a bit more space,' someone suggested. They did that, but to no avail.

'We could take out the door frame?' But it was still no good, the umbrella would not pass through.

No one had actually seen the priest come in with the umbrella. All they knew was he had come in the door and he had left the umbrella in the kitchen. They were baffled: why could they not bring out the contraption the same way he had brought it in? Was it a test of their piety? And had they failed it? Was there some kind of a charm on it that only the priest could break? Was it a magic umbrella?

At last they admitted defeat. They sent the messenger back to tell the priest he must come and get the umbrella himself.

The priest was baffled. What on earth was the problem? He was annoyed that he would have to spend the rest of his day going back out to the rural cottage, but there seemed to be no alternative if he wanted his umbrella.

When the priest arrived, he saw the door off its hinges, and the mess where the door frame was removed. Everyone was watching to see how he would manage where they had failed.

The priest took up the umbrella, closed it and rolled it up. Then he walked out the door. What else could he have done?

THE MUNGRET WASHERWOMEN

The monasteries of Mungret and Lismore could not agree. The one thing most of all that caused friction between them was which school had the higher standard of learning. Each maintained that their students were the more academically adept. At last they agreed to hold a contest to test the literary skill of the students, and the contest would take place at Mungret.

The Mungret scholars were very accomplished but they were still afraid that the Lismore monks would prove themselves superior in some way. They planned to find a way to outdo their rivals. At last they had a brilliant scheme that they would enact on the morning of the contest.

Several of the Mungret monks disguised themselves as washerwomen and gathered on the banks of a stream that ran through the monastery grounds. The Lismore monks would have to pass them on their way to the contest.

Approaching the stream, the Lismore scholars greeted the washerwomen with a wave and a few words about the weather. Speaking in Irish, they asked for directions to the monastery.

They were very surprised when the laundry maids returned their greeting, agreeing that indeed the weather was fine and gave clear and precise directions – in both Latin and Greek.

The Lismore men were convinced there was no point in continuing to the contest. If the washerwomen of Mungret were so well versed in languages, what must the monks be like? They sheepishly made their way back home and quietly conceded the day to Mungret.

TEA LEAVES

The Irish have long loved their cup of tea, indeed many could not imagine a day without it. Most have their preferences. Some insist the pot be scalded first, before the tea leaves are added. Others that only water freshly boiled be used. But there was a time when tea was still a rare delight, drunk only as a special treat. A man who was once the parish priest in Glin told a story of the strangest cup of tea he had ever been served.

When he was a young priest, he was saying a mass in a large country house one day. The owners invited him to stay and have his breakfast with them. He looked forward to that, eating at a smart table. While the mass was going on upstairs, the servants were busy below making the breakfast and preparing the tea.

The priest was very surprised when the servant placed before him a bowl of warm tea leaves. After a while he was able to laugh about the day he taught the servants of the big house how to make a pot of tea.

NOAH AND THE KERRYMAN

In County Limerick, many stories were told about their neighbouring county, Kerry, the crux of these being that Kerry folk were not as smart as Limerick people.

They say that the Kerry people are well used to the rain, and scarcely notice it at all. That is just as well for there are some places in Kerry where it rains all the time.

A long time ago, it was the time of Noah's flood, it had been raining for thirty-five days. The whole of Ireland was covered with water, except for the very top of Carrantuohill Mountain in County Kerry. All the Irish were drowned. No one was left alive except for one Kerryman, who was resting up on the top of the mountain, waiting for the weather to improve. After a while he saw a boat come sailing by. The door of it opened up and out popped Noah, calling, 'Come on away in out of the rain, man.'

'Ah, no,' says the Kerryman. 'Although it is a fine boat you have there, it is hardly worth my while to come on board. Sure, this is only a shower, and it will be dry again shortly.'

SOURCES

'An Early Start': NFCS 523:425. William Morgan. Collector: Michael Richardson
'Nature or Nurture': NFCS 523:487-9. Tim Ryan, Ahane, Lisnagry
'The Priest's Umbrella': NFCS 480:209. Tim Joseph Casey, Glin, Co Limerick
'Tea Leaves': NFCS 480:169 Tim Joseph Casey, the terrace, Glin.
    Ballygiltennan (B), Glin
'Noah and the Kerryman': NFC 1305:124

16

LOVE YOU LARGE, LOVE YOU SMALL

There was a man and his wife lived together in a comfortable house on a fine bit of land. All should have been well between them: they had no worries about money, nor shortage of food, the land was good and their cow gave plenty of milk. But there was one thing that caused trouble between the two: the wife believed that she was too fat. Because of this, she was never happy with her lot. She was always giving out and her poor husband, who honestly thought she was just fine as she was, had his days filled with her endless complaints.

The man would do whatever he could to try to cheer her up. If he had been to market and made a good sale, he would buy her some small trinket: a brooch, or a pin for her hair, perhaps even a new hat. No matter what he brought her, somehow it was never quite enough.

She would say, 'If only I was thinner, that would look so beautiful on me,' or, 'If only I was smaller that would be so lovely with my colouring.'

In her eyes, nothing could ever compensate for her not being as slim as she would like to be. This burned away within her, making her bitter and cross. So whenever her husband tried to make her feel better, or convince her that he loved her regardless, she would cry, and then fly into a rage, and shout at him, as if her large size was all his fault. The poor man was at a loss. Was there nothing he could do to please his wife?

One evening coming home, he was sorely burdened by the thought of the abuse he would get from his unhappy spouse when he'd step in the door. His path took him by the edge of a fort, and to delay the moment, he sat on a big rock by the side of a spring well and lit his pipe. He hadn't been there two minutes, when he heard a voice say:

> 'This well's clear water has the power
> to make the fat slim within an hour.
> A single cup of this clear water will make any body smaller.'

As soon as he heard those words, he leapt up and ran all the way home, desperate to share this news with his wife. She was delighted, and the two danced around the kitchen, laughing and kissing, and happy together for the first time in years.

'You can go to the well first thing in the morning,' he said, hoping to have a pleasant evening at home, now that she was no longer mad with him.

'Not at all. I cannot wait till morning,' she said, fetching a china cup from the dresser. 'I would not sleep a wink for thinking about it. Better to go now!' Out the door she went.

She ran all the way to the well by the fort, then bent down and filled her cup with the clear water. It was cool and sweet as she drank it down, wondering would one cup be enough, as she was so large? Thinking maybe she'd better take a second cup, she filled her cup again, and drank it down. And then a third time.

Suddenly everything around her was changing: trees, rocks, everything was growing bigger and bigger. No, that wasn't it – it was herself that was getting smaller and smaller. First she was the size of a 10-year-old; then a 4-year-old; and then she just kept on shrinking. When she finally stopped shrinking, she was the size of a baby! What was she to do now? She couldn't walk home on her little legs, so she had to stay there for the night.

Wondering what was taking her so long, the husband came to the well to find her. He was very surprised to see the baby by the well, but he knelt down and gently picked her up and carried her home in his arms.

Sad to say, the spring water was not a cure-all for relationship problems! Life in that comfortable house on the fine bit of land continued as strife-ridden as ever. Although she now looked like a baby, the wife was still her old self in all other ways. She still had the angry tongue in her head and regularly gave out to her husband with all the abuse she had used before. She was still not happy with the way she looked and now she was blaming him for it. Could you not have come with me to the well? You could have stopped me drinking too much water! Ah, you fool, you useless …'

Still, he stayed with her until she grew back to a 'normal' size again, which took quite some time. I couldn't swear that she was content with the way she looked even then.

But still he loved her, just as she was, and that was the long and the short of it, or the large and the small of it. And who among us could wish for more than that: to be loved and accepted, just as we are?

SOURCE

NFCS 501:290. Mary Daly, Kilscannel. Collector: Bridie Sheey.
   Árd-achadh School, County Limerick

17

THE BLACK PIG

All around the country, dolmens or ancient stone monuments have often been locally known as 'Diarmuid and Gráinne's Bed'. It is usually said that Gráinne and Diarmuid slept there whilst on the run from Finn MacCool.

However, there is a dolmen in the townland of Ballynagallagh, near Lough Gur, that bears a different name: 'Leaba na Muice', or 'The Pig's Bed'. Its story is about a fabled black pig that once terrorised farmers in this area.

There was once, long ago, an enormous black pig that made its home at the stones of Leaba na Muice. It was a ferocious beast that roamed the countryside doing great damage to any other creature it encountered, whether they were large or small. Even cows, and other animals larger than itself, were often found wounded by the marauding pig. Many of the small farms in the area suffered losses that they could little afford.

At last the people decided that something must be done, and they must take the offensive against the beast. They sent out a call far and wide for all who longed to see an end to this destruction to meet at Cnoc Áine, about 4 miles from Leaba na Muice. A large crowd responded, all determined to drive the black pig from their lands. They gathered on the hill, bearing whatever tools or weapons they could lay their hands on. They carried forks, knives, hatchets, old swords and pikes.

But where should they start? The black pig had done its damage over a very wide area, and there were many places thought to be its lair. As one of those was close to Cnoc Áine, they decided to start the hunt there.

They spread out in a long line and set off together, marching northwards in the direction of Lough Gur. They thrashed their way through every thicket, searched every woodland copse, looked under the shelter of overhanging rocks, but nowhere could they see a trace of the ferocious creature.

When they neared the stones of Leaba na Muice, the black pig, followed by four squealing *bonhams*, emerged from under the heavy flagstone that served as its roof. The old mother pig fixed the farmers with a fierce stare. Lifting her head, she showed them her long tusks, moaning and snorting and pawing the earth beneath her, all that time keeping her young safely behind her. Close up, the creature was even more terrifying than she had seemed before, and the farmers fell silent, all petrified at the sight.

Whilst the black pig held the mob frozen with her gaze, three of the four young pigs made a sudden run for freedom, heading in a northerly direction. The fourth *bonham* retreated into the *leaba* and hid there. Later, when the army of farmers had passed by in pursuit of her mother and sisters, she also ran off, but in a southerly direction.

The old sow held the hunters at bay with her wild cries as long as she could. Only when she thought her young ones had a safe distance between them and the armed men, did she turn and run. By this time the men had slowly encroached, and had her almost surrounded. There was still one small gap in the circle of angry men, and the black pig fled in that direction. As she ran towards the north, she turned her head and in a fierce growl she uttered these words over the pursuers: 'Woe to the people between Cork and Limerick!'

The three *bonhams* who had headed north stayed together, their mother bringing up the rear. Before long they had outrun their pursuers, and were now safe from any immediate danger. The young pigs separated, each taking a different direction. One forged its path westward to Connacht; the second went east

towards Leinster; the third had the longest journey, and fled north
to Ulster; the fourth had already headed south. Each *bonham* had
gone to one of the four provinces of Ireland.

As for the great sow herself, she ran towards the city of Limerick,
and from there she faced north-east and, keeping a parallel path
to the Shannon river, she kept on running until she reached Sligo.
She ran in the valleys, keeping to woods and wherever she might
find cover.

They say that traces of her journey are sometimes still known as
'The Valley of the Black Pig'.

Source

NFCS 516:257, John Clancy, Grange, County Limerick

18

THE SIEGE OF KNOCKLONG

Knocklong was once known as Druim Damhghaire, 'The Ridge of the Oxen', but now it takes its name from Cnoc Luinge – 'The Hill of the Encampment'.

When Cormac Mac Airt was High King of Ireland, during the third century, he demanded an arduous double tribute from the people of Munster. When Fiacha, the King of Munster, refused to pay twice the usual tax, Cormac decided to teach him a lesson. He set off from Tara to invade Munster and force the new regime upon them. It took his army five days' march to reach the hill of Knocklong and there Cormac's army took up their position, while Fiacha's army camped below at Glenbrohane. The fighting went on for days, but with no progress.

Then Cormac called his druids for help and they cast spells on all the spring wells, rivers and lakes in the area. Every lake, stream, river and well within miles became dry. The people of Munster began to suffer from the drought and the siege. All seemed lost, until King Fiacha called on the help of Mog Roith, a Kerry druid, who had learned magic from masters of the elements in the east.

Mog Roith had taught Fiacha as a boy and had foreseen that one day the army of the north would March against Fiacha, and there would be no one to help him, unless he himself would come to his aid.

Fiacha asked what his fee would be. The druid's answer was: 'A hundred white cows in milk; a hundred fat pigs; one hundred oxen; one hundred racehorses; the hand of a beautiful woman for a wife; and the land of my choice within Munster.'

It was a high price to pay, but what else could Fiacha do but agree?

Mog Roith set off in his war chariot, piled high with weapons, bringing his servant and disciple, Canvore, with him. He cast his magical silver spears into the earth and so caused the waters of Munster to flow again. The first spring to be restored was given the name Tober Canvore, as the disciple had cast that spear. The people rejoiced that they could drink and refresh themselves again.

Then Fiacha asked Mog Roith to flatten the hill of Knocklong. 'It insults me that I have to look up towards the hill where Cormac's army sits and mocks me.'

'Face me towards the hill' said Mog Roith. Then he spoke words of power and he grew as tall as the hill itself, his head as wide and crowned with oak woods. All who saw him in this state were afraid and trembled. He began to blow upon the hill and it shook, the tents of the warriors flapping in the wind. He blew again, and the hill vanished behind grey storm clouds. Cormac's army was in disarray, horses and men running in all directions, as the hill shook and crumbled around them.

When the hill was reduced to dust, Mog Roith called for his poisoned stone and cast it into the river, where it became a giant conger eel, which bound Cormac's champion into nine knots.

Now Cormac called his fairy druids, three fairy women, who transformed themselves into metal sheep, with hardened heads. These strange beasts marched against Fiacha's army. But Mog Roith called for his druidic tools, spoke further words of power, and three giant dogs drove the sheep into a hole in the earth and devoured them.

Cormac now saw surrender as his only way out, but Mog Roith would not accept this. He demanded a contest of fire, druid against druid.

Soon Cormac's fire was built. Mog Roith gave Fiacha's men orders to each bring a handful of rowan wood, while Fiacha was to bring wood from the mountain. Each man shaved a sliver of wood from his spear shaft and Mog Roith mixed these with butter to form a ball. The butter ball was set alight and the flames rose high into the air with a roar.

Mog Roith made ready his chariot, donned his bull's hide and his winged bird's mask, and flew, chanting and fanning the flames.

The fire moved fiercely towards the north, driving Cormac's army and his druids before it. Cormac retreated to the north, without his taxes, never to return.

SOURCE

www.shee-eire.com/magic&mythology/myths/Heroes&Heroines/Siege-Knocklong1/siege.htm
Caitlín and John Matthews, *Encyclopaedia of Celtic Wisdom* (Element, 1996)

19

KING OF THE REEKS

There was once a young King of the Reeks who was very fond of hunting wild fowl. He would wander far and wide following the fowl. One day he had travelled so far from home, and climbed so high that he had to sleep that night on the side of a steep high mountain.

When he awoke the next morning, all around him the sea had risen, and lapped at his heels – Noah's flood had come in the night! The King of the Reeks had no choice but to live on the birds of the air, who flew around him on his small bit of land.

One morning when he awoke he found that the waters had receded a little. In the distance he saw a little thatched cottage, and he set off in that direction. All around the cottage, the land was sodden and marshy. Inside he met an old man and an old woman, who were both starving hungry. So the King of the Reeks set traps and brought them wild fowl to eat. He stayed there with them and all went well for some days, until another man came by. The stranger asked if he would play a game of cards with him.

'I will,' said the King of the Reeks, 'but what shall we play for?'

'Let us play for a wish,' said the stranger and they agreed.

They played three rounds and the King of the Reeks won them all. 'So, what is your wish?' asked the stranger.

'I wish I had a wife,' says the King of the Reeks.

The stranger went away and came back with three of the love-liest women the sun and moon ever shone on. Beautiful as they were, still not one of them won the heart of the King of the Reeks. The stranger went off and returned with three plain, ugly women.

The king chose one of these to be his wife and soon he learned that she was under an enchantment.

The new wife pleaded with the King of the Reeks not to play cards again with the stranger, for he would surely lose this time. The stranger came on a second day and asked for another game, and the king agreed. They played three rounds, and the king won them all again. 'So, what is your wish today?' asked the stranger.

'I wish I had land of my own.'

'When you wake up tomorrow, if you look around, there you will see your land around you.'

The stranger came again on a third day. Again the king's wife pleaded with him not to play, but he ignored her warning. This time the King of the Reeks lost the game, and had to ask the stranger, 'What is your wish?'

The stranger wished for, 'The sword of lightning from the eastern part of the world where the sun and moon have never shone,' and he gave the King of the Reeks just one week to fetch it for him.

Next morning the King of the Reeks had to tell his wife that he had played and lost the game this time.

'Now we must go back to my father's place,' he said and they set off across the fields. He was the faster walker and soon she was some distance behind him. When he waited for her to catch him up, instead of his plain wife he saw the most beautiful woman that the sun and moon ever shone on! Now he waited for her to walk beside him, helped her over the ditches and hedges, and he found her conversation was bright, lively and very interesting. At last they saw his father's home in the distance.

The wife gave him a bridle. She told him to take it out into a field and bring back the first pony that put its head into the halter. There came a weak sickly beast, nudging its head toward the halter, but the King of the Reeks quickly shooed it away. He came back to his wife with nothing.

'Why did you chase that sick little pony away? You were to bring the first pony to put its head in the halter. Go back and fetch him.'

He went back out to the field and led the sickly pony back to his wife.

'Now climb on his back and he will carry you to the castle. Listen to what he tells you, for though he looks weak and foolish, he knows many things.'

He rode off on the pony's back and it took him to the castle. When the King of the Castle asked what had brought him here, he replied, 'A wise wife, admired by many, and a smart little pony.'

The King of the Castle declared, 'Now you are here, we will have a game. I will hide and you must find me.' Saying this, he disappeared, quick as a flash.

The King of the Reeks spoke to his pony, who told him, 'You will find him hiding in an apple in the garden.' The pony described exactly where in the garden the apple lay. He walked along the garden paths, found the apple, brought out his knife and was about to cut it in two, when out leapt the King of the Castle.

'Very good! You found me easily that time. Now I must hide again and you must find me.'

This time the pony told him that the King of the Castle was hiding in an egg inside a grey duck. He took his gun and went out to hunt fowl by the water's edge. He saw the big grey duck, raised his gun and was about to shoot, when out leapt the King of the Castle.

'Aha, very good! You found me easily that time. Now I must hide a third time and you must find me.'

This time the king hid himself in a ring on his daughter's hand. The young fowler found the ring and was about to break it in two when out leapt the King of the Castle.

'Aha, very good! You found me easily that time. You are surely the finest young man I have ever met. In reward, you may have my daughter as a bride.'

Despite protestations from the King of the Reeks, a wedding was quickly arranged. 'Now, sit ye up in the carriage with your bride.'

The King of the Reeks refused. 'No, I would rather ride there on my own pony.'

They travelled on until they came to a great mansion. 'Oh dear, I seem to have misplaced my gloves!' said the young King of the Reeks.

'You are very welcome to borrow mine,' says the King of the Castle.

'But I bought them especially for the wedding. I will just go back and fetch them.'

The young King of the Reeks went out and his pony spoke to him. 'Do you see that flat stone covering the well? The sword of lightning is hidden beneath the stone.' The pony kicked the stone with his heels and it moved. There was the sword!

The King of the Reeks was making his way back home with the sword when the King of the Castle came riding on his war horse. A battle ensued and the young King of the Reeks used the sword of lightning to cut off his enemy's head.

He could now return to his wise young wife and they lived together happily for some time. When he began to go fowling again, his wife warned him that she was afraid something bad would happen soon. He was out hunting wildfowl one day when a giant with nine heads, nine bodies and nine legs came and stole away his wife. When the king reached home, he was surprised to find her gone. He asked his pony if anything strange had happened while he was away. 'A giant with nine heads, nine bodies and nine legs came and took your wife away with him.'

'Then I will not rest until I find her and bring her back again!'

He journeyed far and wide, in search of his wife, on land and by sea. At last he sailed to an island, where he stopped for food and water.

'Oh you are not at all like the fellow who came here yesterday,' said the island man.

'What was he like, this man?'

'He was a giant of a man, with nine heads, nine bodies and nine legs, a foul temper and no friend of mine was he.'

'That sounds like the foul fellow who stole away my wife!'

'Well, if you should ever need my help, call on me. My name is Wolf of the Forest.'

The King of the Reeks sailed on, stopping on another island. Here the same thing happened, the island man describing the giant and saying, 'If you should ever need my help, call on me. My name is Hawk of the High Cliffs.'

On a third island, the same happened again, the island man describing the giant and saying, 'And if you should ever need my help, call on me. My name is Trout of the Blue Rock'.

He sailed on. Landing on another island, he saw his wife fetching water from a well. How glad he was to see her! 'How did you come here? Are you well? Have you been treated badly?'

'It was a giant with nine heads, nine bodies and nine legs who stole me away and brought me here, but no, he has not harmed so much as a hair of my head. He holds me here by an enchantment, and his own life is secured by magic spells.'

'Tell me, how is his life secured? How can I slay him and bring you safely home?'

'The giant is a foolish and boastful man. He told me the secret of how his life is secured. There is a tree by the door. Within that tree there is a wolf. Within the wolf there is a duck. Within the duck there is an egg. The giant's life is within that egg, and none can reach it there. The tree can only be felled by the sword of lightning, and his brother has the sword.'

The young King of the Reeks brought out the sword of lightning and hacked down the tree. When the wolf leapt out of it, he called on the help of Wolf of the Forest. Wolf of the Forest slew the wolf, and out ran the duck. He then called on Trout of the Blue Rock, who slew the duck. When he saw the egg fly out, he called on Hawk of the High Cliff, who caught it and gave it to his wife.

The good wise wife cracked open the egg, and the giant with nine heads, nine bodies and nine legs shrieked and writhed on the ground before them until he was dead.

The King of the Reeks and his wise young wife went home and lived happily together all their days.

SOURCE

NFCS 487:185. Patrick Dwyer, Ballyrobin. Collector: Nellie Fitzgerald, Ballynacally. Ardagh (C) School

20

OWNEY AND
OWNEY-NA-PEAK

A long time ago, in a time of peace and plenty, there were two young men living in a village near Limerick city. The two were cousins, and both were named Owney. The first, a smart, kind-hearted, handsome, bright young fellow of slight frame, was simply known as Owney. The cousin was a different kind of fellow altogether, and the neighbours christened him Owney-na-peak, which means 'Owney of the nose'. Owney-na-peak's nose was so long and pointed that it could be seen a good five minutes before the man himself would arrive. The people used to say that if you looked at one side of his face, it would be a good morning's walk to get around the nose to catch a glimpse of the other side! Owney-na-peak was a stout, rounded fellow, a strong man, well able to carry the heaviest of weights. He was not very bright and, to be honest, he was a bit of a bully towards his cousin, with whom he worked in partnership.

Both of them were smiths. Not blacksmiths, they were white-smiths, working with tin and other metals, and the finishing off of iron goods. There was plenty of business came their way from the lords of the court and knights and wealthy folk of the city.

One day when Owney was in town he saw a great procession passing through the streets. There were all the lords and ladies, the generals and so on, and amongst them, the king's daughter. She was simply most beautiful young woman Owney had ever seen and his heart just leapt out of his chest at the sight of her.

He was in love and forgot all about the business he was in Limerick to do.

Everyone said that the best way to get acquainted with royalty – as that was what he now dearly wanted to do – was to have money. So Owney started to save all that came his way, hiding it in a place he thought was safe. When he had a few bits of silver put aside, Owney-na-peak found the hidden coins and took them for himself. If Owney protested, then Owney-na-peak would beat him. That was the way it was.

One night Owney's mother called him to her bedside. She was dying and she had something to say to her son. 'You have been been a good dutiful son to me, Owney. Now here is something in reward.' She handed Owney an old china cup. 'Take this china cup to the fair and sell it.'

Owney looked at it. It was just an ordinary china cup, there was even a bit of a chip out of it. But his mother continued, 'There is a fairy gift upon it. Use your wits, keep your eyes open, and let it go to the highest bidder.' She took his hand, 'Bless you, my lovely white-headed boy.'

The next day, Owney buried his mother and the day that followed, he took the china cup and set off for the fair in Garryowen. He walked up and down through the rows of stalls and awnings, looking at the wares for sale. Everything there seemed so fine, that he was quite ashamed to speak out and draw attention to the cracked cup he had to sell. So he just kept on walking from stall to stall, watching the people come and go. When evening was drawing near, a stranger tapped him on the shoulder and said, 'My dear fellow, I have noticed you going back and forth through the fair all day with that cup in your hand. It looks as if you are wanting something. Tell me, what can it be?'

'I am to sell this cup to the highest bidder,' says Owney.

A second man, hearing this, came up for a closer look. 'What is it you are selling?' he said.

'Away with you,' said the first, 'what is it to you? I was looking at it first.'

'Have I not the right to ask its price?' said the second man.

The first man made Owney a sudden offer. 'Here, lad, I will give you this golden piece for your china cup.'

'That cup will never grace your home,' said the second. 'Here, lad, I give you two gold pieces for the cup.'

Another man, hearing the bargaining over the cup, came in. 'I will give you ten gold pieces to take it home with me.'

A lord of the court rode up just then. Hearing the offer of ten gold pieces, he wondered, 'Ten gold pieces for a china cup? It must be a precious treasure,' and he spoke to Owney, 'Here, boy, I will give you twenty pieces of gold. Now give the cup to my servant and let us be done with it.'

'I will give you this purse with thirty pieces of gold,' said another lord, 'if you will give it to me. Let no man outbid me now, or he will feel the edge of my sword!'

'No man am I, but I outbid you, with twenty more pieces!' said a lady of the court.

Owney put the cup into her hand, and took up the fifty gold pieces. He was thinking to himself, 'Fifty pieces of gold for my mother's old chipped cup that wasn't worth one of them! There was a fairy gift all right on that cup, Mother.'

As Owney made his way back home, he thought he had best stop and hide his money, as he knew Owney-na-peak would take all he had and leave him not one gold piece. He dug a hole in the ground and hid all but two pieces there, then went on home.

Owney-na-peak laughed as his cousin came into the house, 'How did you fare at the fair, cousin? Did you get a good price for your treasure?'

'Not so bad at all,' said Owney, sounding well pleased with himself, 'I got two gold coins for it.'

'Let me see those two gold coins!' Owney-na-peak grabbed the money from his cousin's hand, and put it in his own pocket. 'They will be safe with me, Owney-boy. Now tell me, how did you get such a good price for that old china cup that wasn't worth five pennies, if truth be told?'

'Well,' said Owney, thinking quickly of a tale to tell, 'I simply walked about the fair crying, "China for sale!" To the first man who came up to me and asked how much, I told him, "One hundred gold pieces." He bargained me down to two, and that's the whole story.'

Next morning Owney-na-peak took out an old china saucer from the press and set off for the fair, without a word to anyone. He caused a bit of a stir, this big roundy fellow with the long nose, calling around the fair, 'China saucer for sale! One hundred gold coins!'

'Are you daft?' said one man. 'No one will give you a hundred gold pieces for that rubbish! Are you trying to make fools of us? Sure, you'll be sorry you tried that!'

Owney-na-peak ignored him, and called again, 'China saucer for sale! One hundred gold coins!'

A crowd gathered around him, laughing. Then they beat him with sticks and fists and left him lying bruised on the ground.

It was late evening by the time Owney-na-peak reached home. His cousin helped him into the forge, feeling a little guilty for the trouble he'd caused. But then he remembered all the ill his cousin had done him and thought this was his fair revenge.

Owney-na-peak saw things differently. 'You rogue, cousin, for tricking me!' He set two irons in the fire and barred the forge door. 'You will not see the light of day again!' He took the two irons and meant to put out Owney's eyes. Owney struggled and pleaded for forgiveness, but all in vain. Owney-na-peak blinded his cousin and then carried him, still in a faint from the pain, to the bleak hillside of Knockpatrick and left him there under a tombstone.

When he came round, Owney realised that he could now see nothing and might never again. 'What is to become of me? How shall I live now, without my trade? And shall I never again see that beautiful face that stole my heart?'

Owney was about to fall into an even greater darkness than his blindness: a great dark pit of despair. Suddenly he heard something. The sound of cats mewing. It sounded as if all the cats in Ireland were gathering on the hill. Every now and then he felt a cat's tail brush against his face. He hid himself behind the stone and listened as the cats began their council.

One voice spoke out to the mewling crowd, 'Welcome, cats of Ireland! Tortoiseshell, tabby, brown, black, grey, yellow and white, all welcome. The sun is resting in the west and the moon is high.

All humans are in their beds and none can hear us. Listen now, in the name of our master, the king of all cats, to the tale I tell. You know the King of Munster's daughter?'

'Oh, we do,' mewed the cats in unison.

A scrawny little black cat with a dirty face said, 'I sit by the fire of Owney and Owney-na-peak, the whitesmiths, and I have heard young Owney speak of his love for her.'

'Quiet,' said the orator cat. 'What do we care for your Owney and Owney-na-peak? Now, cats, my story is this: last week the king was struck down with blindness and he offers his daughter's hand in marriage to the man who can cure him. Now as cats, we all know the cure for blindness is to walk the rounds and take the water from the well at Barrygowen. I warn ye all this night to guard our secret, for there is a man coming to try his skill, a great-grandson of Simon Magus. It is he, and he alone, who must use the water and marry the princess. No other man must hear of it. He promises us a feast of the fattest mice that ever walked on the ground.'

The cats all clapped and purred and mewed, did a little cleaning, then scampered off down the hill homewards, where they took up their places by the hobs.

Owney waited until there was no more sound of cats, then went to the Barrygowen well. He found his way by groping touch to the road and by the sound of the waves from the Shannon. He walked around the well, then stooped to take the water. Rubbing his eyes, he looked up and saw the sun rising in the east! He gave a hearty, 'Thanks to God – and the cats!' then made his way back to the forge.

Owney-na-peak was astonished to see him, and with his sight restored. 'Well, cousin, I did not expect to see you today.'

'I have come to thank you,' said Owney, holding up two coins he had dug up from his hiding place. 'For if you had not put out my eyes, I would never have got these two pieces of gold. Perhaps, if you are brave enough to let me put out your eyes and lay you in that same place, you might have the same good fortune?'

'Ah, now, there's no need for blinding at all,' said the cousin, 'but if you will put me in that same place, I am willing to try my fortune tonight.'

Owney noticed the cat, the scrawny black with the dirty face, pause in her cleaning and look up with sudden attention. He signalled to his cousin to say no more. When the cat got up and left the forge, he closed the door behind her, and agreed to take Owney-na-peak to the hill and place him under the same tombstone that very night. The cat, meanwhile, was peeping in through a broken pane of glass in the window, listening closely.

That night Owney brought his cousin to Knockpatrick Hill and laid him under the stone. Owney went on to rest at Shanagolden for the night, ready to see what would happen by morning.

Meanwhile, resting in the darkness under the stone, Owney-na-peak heard the sound of cats gathering on the hill. He overheard them greeting each other, asking after the kittens and so on. At length the orator cat called out for silence, and then began his speech. 'Welcome, tortoiseshell, tabby, brown, black, grey, yellow and white, all welcome. The sun is resting in the west and the moon is high. All humans are in their beds, and none can hear us.'

'Stop! Be wary, for there was a human here last night. He heard all we said and he has a bottle of Barrygowen water above his chimney today. I saw it myself in the house of Owney and Owney-na-peak. There is a human here again tonight and he is hiding under a big stone!'

The cats began to scream and mew like banshees. They flew about the hill with their claws out, seeking the intruder. When, at last, they spotted his nose peeping out from the tombstone, they set upon him with a vengeance, and tore him to shreds.

In the morning, Owney found his cousin's bones scattered all over the hill. He thought, 'He showed little kindness towards me in his life, but still, he was my cousin.' So he gathered up the bones into a sack, and brought them to the Barrygowen well. He walked the rounds and threw the bones into the well. No sooner done, than Owney-na-peak scrambled out of the well, and seeing his cousin there, punched him full in the face. Owney fell to the ground, and his brute of a cousin pushed him into the sack, meaning to drown him in the Shannon. Carrying the sack was heavy work, and the wicked cousin stopped for refreshment in a public house. He left the sack down by the wall, warning Owney to be still and silent. Owney tore a little window in the sack and looked out. He saw an old man in the corner by the fire. 'Oh, let me die,' said the old man, 'for I have no one to care for, nor anyone to care for me. It would be best if I were dead.'

Owney thought to himself, 'What is it? Someone is looking for death, but cannot find it, while here I am destined for death, but do not wish it.' He began to sing quietly:

> *'To him that tied me here, be thanks and praises given.*
> *I'll bless him night and day, for sending me to heaven.'*

'What did you say? Will you let me take your place in that bag, so that I might die and go to heaven in your place?' said the old man.

'I will for sure,' said Owney, 'if you will untie the bag and let me out.'

The old man released him but Owney suddenly felt bad about fooling the old man. He noticed a pig hanging from a rafter in the kitchen, and brought that down. To the old man's surprise Owney tied the pig into the sack instead.

'Now go home, old fellow,' he said. 'You came close to death today, but were saved.'

The two left the house together, and Owney made his way home to the forge and dug up four gold pieces from his hiding place.

Later, having taken his fill, Owney-na-peak came back to the kitchen and took up his sack, without noticing any difference in its load. Hefting it over his shoulder, he climbed onto a high rock and threw the bag into the salt water.

When he reached the forge, wasn't he surprised to see Owney standing at the open door? He thought it must be a ghost, and was reaching for the holy water. Owney looked happy and bright, and said to his cousin, 'So many good turns you have done me in this life, cousin, but this last is the greatest yet. Under the sea I found a great palace, and a cave filled with treasure! These four gold pieces are but a fraction of what I could carry.'

'I wouldn't mind a bit of that gold!' said Owney-na-peak. 'Will you throw me into the water so I can get me some gold? But tell

me, how did you get here before me? I did not stop on my way
from Knockpatrick.'

'There is a shortcut beneath the waves,' said Owney.

So Owney tied his cousin into the sack and he threw it onto a
cart that was passing that way and heading for Foynes.

When he reached the rock, he very nearly threw the sack into
the water, but his conscience got the better of him. He spied a little
boat that was due to board a great ship heading for foreign parts.
He made a bargain with the ship's captain and carried the sack on
board, leaving it there. Owney was never bothered again by his cruel
cousin, who is most likely still sailing the seven seas to this day!

Owney stopped at Barrygowen well for another bottle of its
healing water. On his way home, he called into the tailor's to buy
a new suit of clothes. Next morning he scrubbed himself well,
combed his hair, put on the new suit, and set off for Limerick city.

He walked up to the palace gate and knocked boldly.

'What do you want?' called the guard.

'I am a doctor come from foreign parts to cure the king's blindness. Take me to him this minute,' said Owney.

'A warning, friend. Did you not see all the heads above the gate?
They are from doctors before you, who tried and failed.'

'I am not afraid. Take me to the king!'

The guard led him to the king, who warned him again of what
would happen if he should fail. He also reminded him of the great
prize if he should be successful. Owney's heart beat faster as he
thought of the princess whom he had loved for so long.

He put the bottle of well water on the ground before the king,
then, on his knees, he made his rounds about it. He took a little
water in his hands and rubbed it into the king's eyes. At once,
the king could see again.

The king commanded that Owney should be made up like
a king's son, and he called for his daughter to meet her suitor.
The princess came reluctantly, for who among us is happy to be
given as a prize, rather than to choose for herself? But when she
saw the man to whom she was promised, her heart melted a little
at the handsome sight of him in his finery, bearing gold and jewels.

'But,' she wondered, 'has he wit as well as looks?' So she set him two questions to be answered the following morning:

'What is the sweetest thing in the world?

What are the three most beautiful objects in the creation?'

Owney puzzled over her questions, but he was a bright fellow, and soon had his answers quite clear.

Next morning, trumpets sounded as they brought him before the princess. She sat in a gilded throne near her father, all dressed in white silk, with pearls in her hair.

There was silence as Owney stood before her to give his answers.

'It is salt!' he said to the first question. The princess smiled, as he had judged well, for it is salt, and not sugar, that gives savour to all we eat, and makes life all the sweeter.

'And the three most beautiful things in the creation – what are they?' she asked.

'A ship in full sail, a field of wheat in ear, and …'

The princess smiled and nodded at him. No one could quite hear what the third beautiful thing was, although the princess blushed and her ladies in waiting giggled behind their hands. Many said that even the highest judges in the land might not have spoken so wisely and well.

The king embraced Owney as his new son and presented him to his daughter. She was delighted that her husband-to-be was both handsome and clever. They were married the following day, and within a year the princess was definitely one of the most beautiful objects in all creation!

SOURCE

Gerald Griffin's story of the same name, in *Fairy and Folk Tales of Ireland*, W.B. Yeats

21

THE RIVER SHANNON

The River Shannon, at 240 miles, is the longest river in Ireland. It flows from the Shannon Pot, its source in County Cavan, all the way to the Atlantic Ocean, passing through many counties and forming three great lakes on its way: Lough Allen, Lough Ree and Lough Derg. The Shannon estuary runs from Limerick city and separates County Limerick from County Clare to the north. There was once a strong salmon fishing industry in the estuary.

THE SHANNON MERMAID

The mermaid is a beautiful creature: her upper body is human, but instead of legs, she has the tail of a fish. She is a creature of the water, whether lake, river or sea. Some say that seven years of bad luck will befall any man who spies a mermaid. She has often been sighted sitting on a rock, combing her long hair. Should a man dare to steal her golden comb, she is likely to wail outside his window, causing him great unease, until it is returned to her. While water is her natural element, she becomes more human when she reaches the shore, and she can live quite happily on land. If a man should get hold of her cloak (sometimes it is her red cap or hood) then she is compelled to go with him and must remain in human form until she recovers it. Although mermaids do not complain about life on land, most seem to harbour a longing for their watery home, and will find it impossible to resist this should they rediscover their cloak.

There was a young fisherman living with his mother in a cottage near Carrigogunnell. He was doing all right for himself at that time, and had his own boat. One day as he was walking down to the shore he saw a mermaid sitting upon a rock, quite close to where his boat was tied. She did not seem at all afraid of him and she made no move to go as he approached. Instead, she watched the fisherman with great curiosity as he walked towards her. Emboldened by her interest in him, the fisherman greeted her, and said a few words about the weather and the price of fish. What else would you talk about when you meet a beautiful fish-woman, and the sight of her has your tongue tied in knots? She did not answer him, but looked into his eyes and smiled.

Just then her cloak fell from her shoulder and landed on the rocks. He bent down to pick it up, meaning to hand the cloak to the mermaid. But as soon as his hand touched her cloak, the mermaid's

tail disappeared, and in its place were two legs. She had become all human, all woman. She reached out her hand and he helped her to stand and climb down from the rocks to the shore path. He thought she was the loveliest woman he had ever seen. The fisherman asked her if she would come home with him, and she agreed.

He brought her home to meet his mother, who thought her a fine young thing. They were married as soon as it could be arranged. What would be the point in delaying? On the eve of the wedding his mother had a word of advice for her son. 'That cloak she had when you first saw her, you must hide it. Put it somewhere that she will never find it. If she should ever come upon her cloak again, you will be very sorry.'

The fisherman took his mother's counsel to heart and hid the mermaid's cloak in a secret place. He told no one where it was and the cloak was never mentioned again. He hoped that they would grow old together happily in that cottage near the shore.

They lived together with his mother. All was well: the fisherman was happy and his new wife seemed content. She worked in the house and the garden, at the mending of nets, the cooking and cleaning, as if she had never been a creature of the sea. She took to life on the land the way a duck takes to the water. It was as if she had known no other life.

One evening a boy came to the cottage with a message from the other fishermen, saying that he must come, and quickly. A school of fish had just gone up the river and they would be sure of a good catch that night.

He sent the boy back with a reply, 'I will be there as soon as I get my nets!'

His nets were stored in a loft above the kitchen. He climbed the ladder in a great hurry, gathering and throwing down his nets. This was too good an opportunity to miss, and he must move quickly if he was to take advantage of it. In his haste he did not notice the mermaid's cloak bundled in amongst his nets.

Down in the kitchen, his wife was busy making a bite for him to eat before he'd leave the house. She saw the cloak come falling down, and what happened next she could not stop, just as a cat cannot ignore a mouse. She reached out, caught it and wrapped the cloak around her shoulders.

Without a backward glance, without a 'Goodbye!' she was out the door before anyone could stop her. Her mother-in-law called to her from the door, 'Wait, my dear. Don't go. Come back!' But it was too late, she had already reached the bank of the river. The fisherman came down the ladder to see what all the shouting was about. His mother brought him to the door, and he saw his own dear wife, a mermaid again, dive into the river.

She was gone, and he would never see her again.

How the River Shannon Got Its Name

A long way from County Limerick where the River Shannon meets the sea, there was once a spring known as Connla's well. Its water was clear and good, and nine hazel trees grew around it. When autumn came, the hazelnuts would drop into the water. The hazel is a tree of knowledge, and its nuts are full of wisdom, so all of that wisdom would seep into the water of Connla's well. The salmon of knowledge swam there, growing in wisdom as he ate the hazelnuts. A guard kept watch over the well night and day, to ensure that no uninitiated man came close who might abuse or contaminate this source of wisdom. All women were forbidden: this wisdom was for men only.

Sionainn, the granddaughter of Manannán Mac Lir, lord of the ocean, was a bright young woman, full of curiosity about the world. If she was forbidden to do something, she took it as merely a challenge to find a way to do it. Sionainn wanted to taste the water of Connla's well. Why should it be kept for the men alone? Surely the women had a right to wisdom too? Surely she herself should have that right?

She had been watching for a long time, and at last one day she found the well unattended. She crept forth and dipped her hand into the water. It was cool and clear, surely it must taste wonderful. She cupped her hands to take a sip. As soon as the water touched her tongue, the well began to bubble and boil. The water rose like a fountain higher and higher into the air, and flowed over. Rushing, foaming, running, the water swept Sionainn off her feet with its force and carried her away. The waters of Connla's well became a mighty river that ran through valleys along the length of the country, bearing Sionainn with it all the way to the sea.

We are not told whether Sionainn found the wisdom she sought: that is a matter for us to ponder. Sionainn became one with the bright silver waters of the river that was given her name, the River Shannon.

Perhaps you will hear her laughter like silver bells as she makes her way back up the river with the tide. Perhaps there are many kinds of wisdom, after all.

Source

'The Shannon Mermaid': NFCS 507:604. Croom (C) School, Croom, County Limerick

A CLOSING LIMERICK

Now that we are closing the pages
On these stories passed down through the ages,
If we do not forget
The truths they beget,
Then we fools may yet become sages.

Also from The History Press

Also from The History Press

HARRY CLARKE